REVERSE MENTORING

REVERSE MENTORING

How Young Leaders
Can Transform the Church
and Why We Should Let Them

Earl Creps

A LEADERSHIP ✣ NETWORK PUBLICATION

JOSSEY-BASS
A Wiley Imprint
www.josseybass.com

Published by Jossey-Bass
A Wiley Imprint
989 Market Street, San Francisco, CA 94103-1741—www.josseybass.com

Readers should be aware that Internet Web sites offered as citations and/or sources for further information may have changed or disappeared between the time this was written and when it is read.

Limit of Liability/Disclaimer of Warranty: While the publisher and author have used their best efforts in preparing this book, they make no representations or warranties with respect to the accuracy or completeness of the contents of this book and specifically disclaim any implied warranties of merchantability or fitness for a particular purpose. No warranty may be created or extended by sales representatives or written sales materials. The advice and strategies contained herein may not be suitable for your situation. You should consult with a professional where appropriate. Neither the publisher nor author shall be liable for any loss of profit or any other commercial damages, including but not limited to special, incidental, consequential, or other damages.

Jossey-Bass books and products are available through most bookstores. To contact Jossey-Bass directly call our Customer Care Department within the U.S. at 800-956-7739, outside the U.S. at 317-572-3986, or fax 317-572-4002.

Jossey-Bass also publishes its books in a variety of electronic formats. Some content that appears in print may not be available in electronic books.

Scripture taken from the HOLY BIBLE, NEW INTERNATIONAL VERSION®. NIV®. Copyright © 1973, 1978, 1984 by International Bible Society. Used by permission of Zondervan. All rights reserved.

Library of Congress Cataloging-in-Publication Data

Creps, Earl G.
   Reverse mentoring : how young leaders can transform the church and why we should let them / Earl Creps.
     p. cm.
   Includes bibliographical references and index.
   ISBN 978-0-470-18898-9 (cloth)
    1. Christian leadership.   2. Christian youth—Religious life.   3. Church renewal.
   I. Title.
BV652.1.C737   2008
253.084'2—dc22

2008027252

Printed in the United States of America
FIRST EDITION
HB Printing 10 9 8 7 6 5 4 3 2 1

Leadership Network Titles

The Blogging Church: Sharing the Story of Your Church Through Blogs, by Brian Bailey and Terry Storch

Leading from the Second Chair: Serving Your Church, Fulfilling Your Role, and Realizing Your Dreams, by Mike Bonem and Roger Patterson

The Way of Jesus: A Journey of Freedom for Pilgrims and Wanderers, by Jonathan S. Campbell with Jennifer Campbell

Leading the Team-Based Church: How Pastors and Church Staffs Can Grow Together into a Powerful Fellowship of Leaders, by George Cladis

Organic Church: Growing Faith Where Life Happens, by Neil Cole

Off-Road Disciplines: Spiritual Adventures of Missional Leaders, by Earl Creps

Reverse Mentoring: How Young Leaders Can Transform the Church and Why We Should Let Them, by Earl Creps

Building a Healthy Multi-Ethnic Church: Mandate, Commitments, and Practices of a Diverse Congregation, by Mark DeYmaz

The Tangible Kingdom: Creating Incarnational Community, by Hugh Halter and Matt Smay

119310

Leading Congregational Change Workbook, by James H. Furr, Mike Bonem, and Jim Herrington

Leading Congregational Change: A Practical Guide for the Transformational Journey, by Jim Herrington, Mike Bonem, and James H. Furr

The Leader's Journey: Accepting the Call to Personal and Congregational Transformation, by Jim Herrington, Robert Creech, and Trisha Taylor

Culture Shift: Transforming Your Church from the Inside Out, by Robert Lewis and Wayne Cordeiro, with Warren Bird

Church Unique: How Missional Leaders Cast Vision, Capture Culture, and Create Movement, by Will Mancini

A New Kind of Christian: A Tale of Two Friends on a Spiritual Journey, by Brian D. McLaren

The Story We Find Ourselves In: Further Adventures of a New Kind of Christian, by Brian D. McLaren

Practicing Greatness: 7 Disciplines of Extraordinary Spiritual Leaders, by Reggie McNeal

The Present Future: Six Tough Questions for the Church, by Reggie McNeal

A Work of Heart: Understanding How God Shapes Spiritual Leaders, by Reggie McNeal

The Millennium Matrix: Reclaiming the Past, Reframing the Future of the Church, by M. Rex Miller

Shaped by God's Heart: The Passion and Practices of Missional Churches, by Milfred Minatrea

The Missional Leader: Equipping Your Church to Reach a Changing World, by Alan J. Roxburgh and Fred Romanuk

The Ascent of a Leader: How Ordinary Relationships Develop Extraordinary Character and Influence, by Bill Thrall, Bruce McNicol, and Ken McElrath

Contents

Part Four: Developing Reciprocity

For my parents, Earl and Jane

About Leadership Network

Since 1984, Leadership Network has fostered church innovation and growth by diligently pursuing its far-reaching mission statement: to identify, connect, and help high-capacity Christian leaders multiply their impact.

Although Leadership Network's techniques adapt and change as the church faces new opportunities and challenges, the organization's work follows a consistent and proven pattern: Leadership Network brings together entrepreneurial leaders who are focused on similar ministry initiatives. The ensuing collaboration—often across denominational lines—creates a strong base from which individual leaders can better analyze and refine their own strategies. Peer-to-peer interaction, dialogue, and sharing inevitably accelerate participants' innovation and ideas. Leadership Network further enhances this process through developing and distributing highly targeted ministry tools and resources, including audio and video programs, special reports, e-publications, and online downloads.

With Leadership Network's assistance, today's Christian leaders are energized, equipped, inspired, and better able to multiply their own dynamic Kingdom-building initiatives.

Launched in 1996 in conjunction with Jossey-Bass (a Wiley imprint), Leadership Network Publications present thoroughly researched and innovative concepts from leading thinkers, practitioners, and pioneering churches. The series collectively draws from a range of disciplines, with individual titles offering perspective on one or more of five primary areas:

1. Enabling effective leadership
2. Encouraging life-changing service
3. Building authentic community
4. Creating Kingdom-centered impact
5. Engaging cultural and demographic realities

For additional information on the mission or activities of Leadership Network, please contact:

Leadership Network
(800) 765-5323
client.care@leadnet.org

Introduction

IT TAKES A CHILD
TO RAISE A VILLAGE

Aaron sprinted out of the darkness like a wide receiver playing a night game. Standing about thirty feet from him on a brightly illuminated platform, I had just begun a talk for a group of youth pastors seated amphitheater-style in the darkness common to these venues. As usual, I planned to speak from my laptop, first because I thought it looked cool (Bill Gates did it); second, because I wanted an icon to demonstrate my freedom from paper; and, third, because I liked the feel of presenting a talk from the same device on which it was composed—so my brand new Sony sat perched on top of a black metal music stand. I also planned to wow this crowd of young leaders by abandoning PowerPoint. What could be more unique than using *no media* for people who spend half their lives exposed to it. The one exception would be my promise to stop at regular intervals to answer questions sent in by text message, a technique based on this group's ultimate technology: the unexpected.

My opening remarks included the confession that I had never spent a single day in youth ministry. Pausing in the silence to let the depth of my ignorance sink in (and praying silently that my eyes would adjust to spotlight-induced blindness), I turned to the right in an attempt to establish eye contact with that sector of the room. As I did, a murmur rose from the crowd to my left, followed by the sounds of footsteps pounding into the carpet from that direction.

Turning back to my left I saw Aaron, a staff member of the group hosting the event. Bolting out of his seat on the front row, he strode toward me with a look of desperation on his face. Then I noticed the movement—the music stand supporting my laptop leaning, then tipping, then falling as if in slow motion. Even though only a few feet away, I felt frozen in place, helpless to prevent the impending destruction of all the documents, slides, graphics, videos, and other files about to disappear in a cloud of silver plastic fragments.

But Aaron started running toward me just in time. Extending his lanky frame to the maximum, he snagged my computer on his fingertips at full stride and ran through the catch as if going for extra yardage. The crowd erupted. Aaron's heroic effort (and superb reflexes) delivered me from a presentation-ending cataclysm. I planned things that seemed "relevant" from the perspective of a midfifties Anglo male, even wearing brand new, thick black, "hipster" glasses. But none of it mattered if Aaron had not been caring enough, or fast enough, to catch my computer as it separated from the tipping music stand. He saved me.

The Ups and Downs of Learning

This book is about the ways in which young and old leaders can serve each other through a relationship called *reverse mentoring*. The concept of mentoring takes its name from *The Odyssey*, the Greek epic in which "Mentor" appears as the person responsible for guiding Odysseus' son as the father goes off to war. In virtually all types of leadership development, this principle of the older and wiser instructing the younger and less experienced remains in force. And for good reason: it works. Paul doubtless mentored the younger Timothy during their travels preaching the good news about Jesus to the Roman Empire of the first century. I take my doctor's advice on medical issues, but he never asks me for the same because only one of us possesses the training and experience worth listening to. In general, then, the kinds of knowledge and wisdom produced by age and experience qualify a person as a mentor.

Reverse mentoring assumes a completely opposite perspective on learning. While acknowledging the proven value of the older-to-younger approach (teaching down), it provides the vital complement of a younger-to-older method (teaching up). Reversing the traditional dynamics feels unnatural to some, especially older leaders like the Baby Boomers who now make up almost half of the American workforce and 60 percent of senior pastors and who have been waiting most of a lifetime to take charge. However, the rate of change in our culture puts younger people in touch with things for which their elders sometimes lack even the vocabulary, suggesting the need to go beyond intergenerational tolerance to reconciliation that leads to a new collaboration.

The young teaching the old represents only an example of reverse mentoring. In truth, I struggled with using the term "reverse" because some infer that the younger person is somehow lesser in value. However, bereft of better wording, I have retained the term used almost universally in both research and practice. Another issue with the topic of generations is the perception that focusing on age differences marginalizes divisions of other kinds. Without question, our world needs multiple forms of reconciliation. The principles involved in reverse mentoring apply across all these cultural fault lines. Generational concerns simply present a familiar case study for grasping the practice, using an example common to a wide variety of leaders.

The key to the relationship, then, is not who is greater or lesser, but the *unlikeliness of* the learning connection. The reversal is as much one of expectations as of position or age. Every culture subsists in part by having boundaries that define it, but these boundaries also serve as barriers that cut people off from each other, making a teaching relationship unlikely. Reverse mentoring (RM) is cross-cultural in that it actually uses the unlikely possibility of a relationship to benefit both parties through mutual learning from honesty and humility.

Spontaneous (and later intentional) teaching-up experiences with a network of twentysomethings created this book. My intrepid wife Janet partnered with me in most of these adventures as our young friends became the faculty of our lives, teaching lessons large and small:

- Cuisine: Hannah, after travels in Europe, tutored Janet in making the perfect cup of tea—just the way the Irish do.
- Research: riding to lunch in his SUV, Justin walked me through how to use my cell phone to perform Google searches using text messaging.
- Connecting: Joel first said the word "Xanga" to me, opening up the world of social networking sites, which led me to MySpace and then Facebook.
- Chatting: multiple mentors cajoled me to set up the online chat (with its inherent multitasking) that I am using to communicate with my friend Donnie as I write this Introduction.
- Resourcefulness: Ryan explained that I could scavenge free wireless signals from the apartment building behind a Starbucks where we sometimes have coffee.

These examples can seem puny compared to the challenges that spiritual leaders face. How will Irish tea reinvent my ministry? However, their significance resides not in the immediate payoff, but in the transforming effect of unlikely relationships and in the potential for learning increasingly significant things later. My friend Ken, for example, managing editor of my denomination's national magazine, received mentoring from Danny, a young man living thousands of miles away that created a global presence for the publication in the blogosphere. After "getting blog literate," Ken describes reverse mentors simply as, "young guys who help the older guys learn young stuff." To put it simply, after many years of taking similar instruction from the young, I cannot imagine my current life or ministry without them.

The Business of Reverse Mentoring

The practice of reverse mentoring claims no inventor or official start date, having been around as long as humans have been learning things. In American culture, the notion of younger teachers for older students found traction in a variety of fields, many of which trace its inception to the example set by Jack Welch at General Electric in the late 1990s. His dramatic mandate that top executives follow his own example by learning communication and e-business technology from younger staffers put the phrase "reverse mentoring" into the vocabulary of the corporate world. Around the same time, Procter & Gamble developed its Mentor Up program designed to solve the problem of attrition among female employees. These and many other examples lent RM cachet sufficient to attract imitators, mainly among those seeking to update the tech skills of their management or increase their awareness of youth culture, hopefully with a corresponding increase in creativity. From there, the principle of teaching up has become influential in almost every imaginable field:

- Security: Ira Winkler teaches companies how to prevent corporate espionage by breaking into their information systems, once stealing plans for a nuclear reactor in less an hour.[1]

- Seniors: BT Rangers, a UK-based Website, recruits young people to teach seniors Internet skills, an accomplishment celebrated on Silver Surfer's Day.

- Teaching: Finland employed thousands of children to teach their teachers about technological issues.

- Legal: the California Bar Association began the Senior Lawyers Project to bring older attorneys into the information age with the help of law students.

- Retail: Proctor & Gamble created a cosmetics company led by net-savvy young people.

From humble beginnings, then, reverse mentoring established itself in the mainstream of business, education, medicine, and many other sectors. After reviewing the practice, journalist Cindy Goodman concludes that, "reverse mentoring is going on in every sector from education to media . . . it is a trend I see increasing."[2] The reason for this growth parallels conventional mentoring: it works, increasing cultural awareness, transferring skills, and stimulating creative thinking.

Despite the widespread commentary, however, very little rigorous evaluation of the practice is available. With some notable exceptions, virtually all of the literature either treats the discipline as one bullet point in a list of mentoring practices (often illustrated by a reference to Jack Welch's program at GE), or simply reviews a chain of positive anecdotes supported by quotes from middle-aged CEOs who learned Internet skills from younger colleagues. Even professional scholars studying the issue struggle to offer specific outcome measurements, with one UK researcher noting, after a massive literature review, that in many studies of mentoring the "analysis goes no further than vignettes and anecdotes," and that, "the evidence on efficacy is always mixed."[3] Nonetheless, the anecdotal evidence is positive enough, and the case studies high profile enough, to continue to attract the interest of organizations in both the for-profit and not-for-profit sectors.

The seeming disinterest in reverse mentoring among ministry leaders creates a void of much greater concern. Unlike their peers in the corporate world, for whom reverse mentoring appears to be a growing trend, Christian leaders seem much less inclined to treat the young as serious sources of information and insight. Scant reference to the discipline appears in either the literature or the conversations of church leaders, which indicates that barriers of some sort are blocking cooperation among the generations. The obstacle may be as simple as the belief that old-to-young learning remains the only valid, biblical method for training and disciple making. It is difficult enough for the mature leader to think of herself as a protégé, let alone the "disciple" of someone half her age.

This attitude, certainly not unique to ministry leadership, may explain why a simple Google search turns up two thousand hits on "mentoring" for every one on "reverse mentoring," while the ratio for a title search on Amazon is 320:1. The lack of reverse mentoring in Christian and other organizations, then, may result from something far more serious: a humility deficit.

"How to" vs. "Why to"

The prominence of these two voids leads me to wonder why a book on this topic has not been written before. The absence of evaluation lends a shallow quality to our understanding of reverse mentoring, defining it as merely a technique, a "best practice" of leaders wanting to be technologically astute or culturally hip. Extending this premise logically, RM involves little more than turning conventional mentoring upside down, and, since we know how to teach down, learning from teaching up offers little or no challenge. Except that the practice seems virtually dormant, perhaps because it implies some uncomfortable realities. Taking instruction from less experienced people in a volunteer organization suggests that the insight and capability of those at the top may be eroding or missing in embarrassing ways. Some leaders respond by evading the discipline. This book is written for those who want to consider embracing it, as a complementary practice to traditional mentoring.

My goal is to prepare spiritual leaders to apply reverse mentoring as a spiritual discipline, a way of experiencing personal formation through exercising the kind of humility that invites younger people to become our tutors. The first section of the book, Facing Reality, confronts the uncomfortable truths (e.g., "I am not cool") that older leaders must consider in order to prepare for Cultivating Spirituality, the subject of the second section, dealing with the spiritual practices (e.g., befriending the unlikely) from which RM draws its life, and which distinguish it from just another value-added business tactic. The third section deals with Experiencing Practicality, identifying three specific examples of reverse mentoring benefits including evangelism, communication, and leadership. The concluding section, Developing Reciprocity, focuses on the development of healthy R-mentoring relationships for individuals and processes for organizations. In the final chapter, Joel and Rachel, two of our young instructors, will describe the experience of teaching Janet and me in their own words.

I have not set out to offer a literature review, a scientific evaluation, or a recycling of business anecdotes, although a bit of each appears here. Neither have I attempted to write a "how to" book. Rather this is a "why to" book. RM is simple to understand and apply, so my main point is to secure the reader's *buy-in* because the methods are accessible to anyone, and the experience is already familiar to any parent of teenage children. Although the young benefit greatly from their role as R-mentors, they are unlikely to offer their services to established leaders for obvious reasons. Older leaders hold the key to the relationship. If you have the openness of heart, the practices are not difficult at all. If you find yourself wanting to try R-mentoring, then I have succeeded.

Also, you will notice the phrase "my friend" appearing over and over, so many times, in fact, that I considered deleting it to avoid annoying the reader. But I could not. In truth, the many young friends mentoring us since early in the twenty-first century have written this book. Consequently, it is a book about relationships, not about methods. The narrative of our relationships runs in the background of everything else contained here. All of the stories are real, as are some of the names. If some of the references and acronyms are unfamiliar, consider getting a reverse mentor right away.

REVERSE MENTORING

Part One

FACING REALITY

1

IDENTITY

"I Am Not Cool"

Janet and I introduce our talk with a simple statement: "You are as cool right now as you will ever be." The students in the young adult discipleship program sitting in the amphitheater before us freeze. Even the pace of surreptitious texting probably drops off. "Right now," we continue, "you are at the very top of the cool curve, and there is only one way to go from there."

A groan rises from the crowd as if from one person.

"We know this in a couple of ways. One of them is that we've met some of your younger brothers and sisters . . . and they don't understand you at all. Your music is nasty, your clothes are weird. And your haircut? Don't get us started. In other words, they already think you're so *over*." Scattered, insincere laughter. "There is another way we know about this: not that long ago, we were you . . . we used to be cool." A muffled gasp. "We wore bell-bottom jeans and worked in coffeehouse ministries the first time—thirty years ago. We used to be cool . . . and now we're not."

Janet and I go on to make the appeal that, because cool shares the shelf life of the average ripe tomato, these students face a hard choice: spend a lifetime pretending their cool remains intact, and along with it their very current cultural knowledge, or realize that a position on the downside of the cool curve creates a fresh opportunity to humble oneself and depend on God. This prospect sobered the young crowd just as it sobers us every day of our ministry lives. Unknowingly, they lived as if their present social identity predicted their future status indefinitely. The two ancient people perched on chairs in front of them served as proof positive that their unspoken assumption was crumbling by the minute. The students knew by observation that this reality arrived for us long ago; they just never expected the same reality to arrive for them so soon. The news unnerved them, just as it unnerves us, ironically giving us all something we truly share, the first step toward reconciling the generations.

This chapter concerns the need for honesty about the leader's identity, expressed pointedly in the statement, "I am not cool." Facing reality on issues like this makes room for the Holy Spirit to grow humility in us, and it offers an essential prerequisite for involvement in many kinds of reverse mentoring. Conventional wisdom assigns the malady of uncoolness almost exclusively to people my age, as if it were a social analog to near-sightedness or baldness. The fragility of cool, however, means that we *all* experience its erosion at varying rates; there are simply those who can admit it and those who cannot. Hopefully, this chapter makes the admission easier and with it increases the likelihood of seeking out mutually beneficial R-mentoring relationships—because cool matters.

The Physics of Cool

A precise definition of *cool* proves elusive with as many descriptions available as there are those willing to write them. But like gravity, the quality itself seems to possess some known features and predictable effects. Writing about the workings of powerful brands, venture capitalist Guy Kawasaki, for example, identifies four attributes of coolness: "Cool is beautiful. Cool is hip. Cool is idiosyncratic. And cool is contagious."[1] His description is not far off from the findings of marketing studies that have identified similar attributes of cool brands, at least in the perception of young adults.[2] As the brand evangelist for the original Apple Macintosh, Kawasaki is in a position to understand the power of cool. Applying his analysis to the iPhone, then, beauty would refer to its aesthetic appeal (the simple, uncluttered shape of the device), hipness would relate to its cultural appeal (the sense of being on the leading edge that comes from using the touch screen), idiosyncrasy would refer to its uniqueness (the dissimilarity of the phone from its peers), and contagiousness would relate to market traction as measured by speed of diffusion (hundreds of thousands shipping in the first few months).

Synergy

Even though these four attributes are fairly easy to describe, the mystery of cool seems to happen when someone experiences beauty, hipness, idiosyncrasy, and contagiousness *simultaneously*, as depicted in a simple grid.

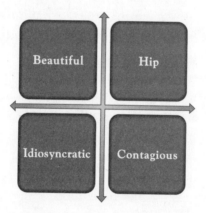

The power of coolness, then, stems in part from a kind of synergy in which the individual elements interact so as to become lost in the overall effect. The aesthetic virtue of an iPod means much less if it lacks uniqueness. Similarly, no amount of hipness compensates for the absence of market appeal in at least some subcultural niche. I suspect this latter factor explains why so many things are cool for such a short period of time.

Finally, nothing is cool until someone says so, because the word itself is by nature and by common usage more of an observation than an inherent quality. If this were not so, an artist thought to be cool could never lose her appeal, but thousands have met this fate. The synergy of the four elements is very much a socially negotiated reality, as is their opposite: the dreaded state of uncool.

This reversal occurs as well when a style or an artist or even a word goes mainstream and in the process violates the principle of idiosyncrasy (uniqueness). Advising me on the mysteries of communicating with college students in northern California, for instance, my friend Rusty, an experienced student pastor, explained them as exposed to "so many worlds" in culture that they reserved respect only for talks (or other things) they recognized as utterly unique. They preferred their truth served raw, or not at all. An aesthetically pleasing, culturally up-to-date talk that proved contagious elsewhere meant little to them if they sensed even minute "generic" traits. That talk might be true but would never be cool, and cool served as the first filter for credibility.

The relationship among the same four attributes also determines some of the variations of cool that appear. Probably no trend, style, or artist possesses all of these characteristics in exactly equal proportions. Thus cool, which ultimately resides in the eye of the beholder, manifests itself in an infinite number of ways, depending on the balance among its four core qualities. After interviewing hundreds of people who seem cool to me, I have concluded that much of what they evoke in others involves a major dimension, a minor dimension, and two intermediate dimensions.

In other words, they tend to express their coolness through one of the four characteristics more intensely than through the other three. One element tends to be their least intense, and the other two are strung out somewhere in between. So the very popular young worship leader is contagious in a major way because his musical gifts and charismatic personality naturally draw the attention of others. At the same time, he

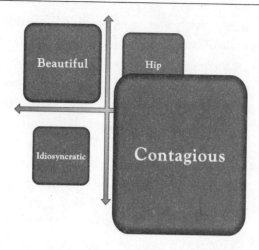

is idiosyncratic in a minor way in that the kind of public persona he represents is readily available in ministries all over the country, on the Internet, and in the Christian music industry. Somewhere in between, in this example, would fall the issues of beauty and hipness. To make this way of thinking about cool more tangible, stop for a moment and place the grid over your own identity as a ministry leader, and ask what might be your major or minor traits. Keep in mind that, because cool exists in the perceptions of others, everyone is cool to someone.

Of course, the number of subtle combinations rapidly approaches the infinite, perhaps suggesting another reason cool seems so easy to spot but so difficult to grasp. Much like "mash-up" art, which combines elements of popular culture to create new forms of expression in video and other media, cool involves more a blend of nuances than a singular idea or style. For example, a panel of experts selected a homemade Superbowl ad—developed at a cost of twelve dollars for the Frito Lay company—as the best advertisement of 2007. The short video literally spawned a thousand imitators and drew four million viewers to a supporting Website.[3] Almost no one could explain in scientific terms why this amateur effort ranked as cool, but four million people can tell you that it does. Experiences like this are consistent with one survey of young adult consumers that found the most important variable in determining the coolness of a brand came down to something as amorphous as its "personality."[4] This subtlety itself develops into part of the appeal, adding a mystique to a new video or communication device or band that leaves its admirers with only one thing to say: "That's cool."

The impossibility of explaining exactly *why* something or someone is cool stands as the ultimate benchmark. Apple's computer technologies, for example, command a devoted following because of their features, but also because of what their devices *don't* feature—a critical aspect of their uniqueness. Andy Ford, a thirty-five-year-old expert in what the marketing world calls "insight," told me recently that "absence" serves Apple well as a primary value, driving the question, "What can we remove?" in the design of every new box.[5] Regardless of their technical merits, then, Apple's one-button or no-button handheld devices experience little competition (yet) in the coolness category. The message is unmistakable: if Apple's style is this much cooler, its hardware must be that much better.

Fragility

The very power of cool also suggests some of its intrinsic limits. Most obvious among these stands the challenge of transporting one culture's cool to another. With the globalization of the world's marketplace and the daily expansion of the Internet economy, ideas, people, and trends spread across national boundaries like never before. The dissemination of an idea that might have taken many months just two generations ago now occurs in hours, or minutes. Attempts by totalitarian regimes to limit access to the Internet on the part of their citizens indicate the mass ideas can take on when they, like physical objects, travel at high speeds. Cool travels through the same channels, catalyzing global audiences for brands such as

Diesel, musical forms such as hip hop, and media sharing sites such as Flickr.com. Paradoxically, cultures so responsive to hip hop that they begin producing their own version of it simultaneously filter out other ideas and media types. My young friend Joel, for example, warned me one day to get rid of my pleated, cuffed slacks because they fell into the category of "old man pants." At the time, flat front slacks apparently blunted the indignities of age more effectively. Another young leader joked that a meeting of Boomers he attended looked like a "Dockers convention." In this context, an age difference proves sufficient to make things that seemed cool to me untranslatable into the cultural language of my younger peers. The underlying issue, of course, is the association of cool with *new*, an equation that applies to more than clothing, and one that further undermines the permanence of anything or anyone perceived as possessing either.

A second kind of fragility results from the way coolness divides people as much as it unites them. One church visitor thoroughly identifies with the vibe of a Sunday morning experience, while a person in the next row is unmoved, and someone else feels repulsed. To create cool means to create boundaries, regardless of the venue. Pop culture specialist John Weir writes in the introduction to an annual *Catalog of Cool*: "Like America, it's tricky, schizophrenic, both democratic and elite. 'You're cool' means 'you're in,' one of us." But if someone qualifies as in, then someone else by definition remains out.[6] One journalist discovered the force used to defend these borders when she created a profile page on the social networking site Facebook, already the hugely popular Internet community of her teenage daughter's peer group. She received this response after messaging her daughter the first time: "Everyone in the whole world thinks its super creepy when adults have facebooks." Out of this struggle, a not-old mom, who knows technology and family issues well enough to write on them for the *New York Times*, concludes, "Although I feel like the same precocious know-it-all cynic

I always was, I suddenly am surrounded by younger precocious know-it-all cynics whose main purpose appears to be to remind me that I've lost my edge."[7]

To some extent, then, cool as a feature of social groups constitutes a fraternity with fairly strict admission requirements screening out some (often older) people at least on some issues. The kinds of identity that depend on the circle of cool also depend on keeping the circle intact. If everyone is cool, no one is, and so the more intense the cool factor, the smaller the circle, creating the paradox of admirers unable to become imitators, like the throngs of fans singing along with Bono at a U2 concert but more likely to be struck by a meteorite than to become a rock star themselves. Closer to home sits the church member present on Sunday out of admiration for the pastor's oratory, yet struggling through a desperate life, untransformed by the thirty-minute talking cure the minister presents each week.

A third limitation on the phenomenon of cool stems from the paradox that real cool requires some degree of unawareness, what Weir refers to as an "unconscious grace." He goes on to lament that, after starting on the edges of culture in venues such as the jazz music scene of the 1930s and then the early days of rock and roll in the 1950s, cool found such a place in the mainstream that: "Our country is committed to an economy of cool. . . . Now it's used to sell stuff. Cars, music, blue jeans, underarm deodorant: turn on the television, everything's cool. Every prime-time star and talk-show guest, dressed in black, void of body fat, confessing a passion for guitar bands and underdog ball clubs, is totally cool. . . ."[8]

A strong proof of this observation takes the form of the cottage industry developing to help both companies and nonprofits find and maintain the cool factor in their brands and organizations. In the mid-1990s, for instance, then-dominant America Online (AOL) hired Kathy Ryan to serve as the "VP of Cool," heading up a "Cool Team" tasked with developing the kind of sites needed to keep AOL on the front edge of Web innovation.[9]

Fast Company featured Ryan in the magazine's very first issue. But today, AOL's customer base is one-third of what it was at the beginning of this century. An Internet-based trend-watching firm offers another approach, called "Cool School," designed to offer "a complete immersion into the entertainment, brands, and activities that are shaping the lives of young people at the moment." For a fee, the student digests such experiences as creating a Facebook profile, being massacred by sixteen-year-olds playing the Halo 3 video game, shopping in high-end boutiques, visiting a "secret" restaurant, or socializing in a hipster club. In spite of this variety, the materials presented change constantly because cool is a moving target.[10]

Aware that their organizations live or die according to something as quixotic as the "personality" of a wristwatch or soft drink, business enterprises use cool as a marketing tactic. In their first half of 2007, the top ten prime-time televisions programs in the United States served as the platform for seventeen thousand product placements. Whenever the camera zooms in on the watch worn by a young superhero until the logo comes into focus, a corporation positions its brand as cool by associating with media personalities perceived as representing the trait. But a dilemma results: as with humility, no sooner do I become aware of cool than it changes into something else, something more like a style that I put on to present myself in a certain way. I sometimes meet leaders my age at conferences dressed in dark clothing, freeze-frame hairstyles, and long-strapped messenger bags mimicking the look of Midwestern young adults. On a twenty-year-old, those artifacts seem native and natural (even though short-lived), but on my peers they seem like affectations, fashions designed to do for our image what Botox is supposed to do for our faces. Leaders using icons of coolness for personal marketing feel "with it," but to others they resemble aging celebrities victimized by too many self-inflicted plastic surgeries. As the effort to achieve a certain look overshadows the reason for looking that way, the fragility of cool catches up with them.

The Marketplace of Cool

The concept of cool, rooted in the twentieth century, persists into the twenty-first perhaps with even greater strength drawn from the dominance of pop and business cultures. The former revels in cool as a core element of personal identity and group cohesion, while the latter uses it as part of marketing strategies designed to associate goods and services with the vibe found in pop culture. Documentary filmmaker Douglas Rushkoff points out in *Merchants of Cool* that a symbiotic relationship between the pop and corporate sectors entices teens and young adults to think of themselves as the architects of cultural icons that actually originate out of marketing research done by huge conglomerates.[11] Specifically, he depicts a very successful campaign to sell Sprite as the product of a carefully orchestrated covert arrangement involving the media companies producing hip hop, Coca Cola, and marketing firms who study how products catch on among teenagers. For Rushkoff, cool is owned, used, and sold by corporate powerbrokers. Having originated on the margins of culture, this experience has become a tactic of the powerful, a "best practice" of business leaders. Cool is now a product *itself*, with a global reach and market cachet. The culture of cool depends first and foremost on the commodification of its primary ingredient. Just as in pop culture, where nothing is cool until someone says so, in the marketing arena millions of dollars are spent on elaborate campaigns to persuade someone to do just that. Sprite is not the real product; cool is.

It comes as little surprise, then, that the value placed on this sort of mystique persists among us as other, related notions come and go. Lucas Conley, writing for *Fast Company*, graphically depicts the dominance of *cool* as an adjective, compared to other terms competing in the brutal marketplace of pop culture.[12]

Recent and doubtless short-lived updates to Conley's chart (*sick, hot, nice*), some of which receded into history long ago in certain parts of the country, only make the remarkable staying power of *cool* more dramatic.

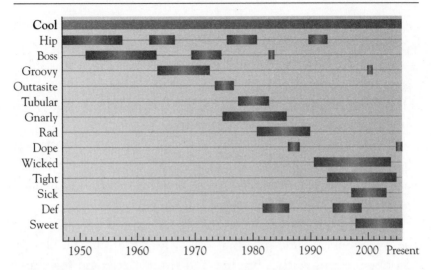

| | 1950 | 1960 | 1970 | 1980 | 1990 | 2000 Present |

(labels, top to bottom: Cool, Hip, Boss, Groovy, Outtasite, Tubular, Gnarly, Rad, Dope, Wicked, Tight, Sick, Def, Sweet)

"A Craving for Cool" by Lucas Conley from FAST COMPANY. Copyright 2006 by Mansueto Ventures LLC. Reproduced with permission of Mansueto Ventures LLC in the format Tradebook via Copyright Clearance Center.

The permanence of cool as both a unique vibe and a marketable commodity simply exceeds the ability of older leaders to emulate it on either level. Like stockholders in a company going under, we possess symbols (stock certificates) that once held value for good reason, but ink dried up on paper means nothing unless it represents a profitable enterprise. As we age, our cool simply goes out of business a day at a time. The pattern does not fall along neat generational lines. One young friend who works with teenagers described herself as positioned "in that weird gap between the two generations . . . it's tricky sometimes because there are times when I feel really old and separated from my students and times when I feel like I know what's going on . . . and other times when I just don't get the way they think!" From this gap, building a bridge to a distant ninth grader meant using the animated television program *The Simpsons* as the common ground. Another friend interviewing a nineteen-year-old for a class project, received a poignant account of his journey away from faith and then reflected in an e-mail to me: "i am learning about track and field trip hop (i hope i got that right), realizing that i need to become more technically proficient with a macbook pro (you should see what he's done with imovie, garageband, and iphoto), and wanting to be a good friend/big sister to a generation that is half my age. (yikes!!! when did THAT happen??) so fun. really—SO INCREDIBLY FUN and humbling and engaging and eye-opening."

These ministry leaders, both about half my age, already feel the pressure. Perhaps the erosion of cool accelerates with each year, but even if not, leaders must prepare to say the dreaded words "I am not cool" at younger and younger ages.

This drop in market value (easily recognized by veterans of the experience) came into high relief for Janet and me during a coffee meeting with a brother and sister, Katie and Josh, and their father, Gary, a friend and fellow minister. Almost right away, the subject of tension between Xers (born 1965–1976) and Millennials (born 1977–2002)[13] somehow arose. Intrigued by this seldom-discussed issue, we started asking questions. Katie (an Xer) immediately commented that she and Josh experienced this decaying market position and the resulting generational stress in four very real ways:

1. The beauty gap: Katie felt the impact of the rift when she coached cheerleaders at a university: "I found out that I was not cool." At one point, the younger girls even approached her with an unthinkable question: "Can we do your makeup for you?" These Millennial girls (only a few years her junior) preferred a different, more recently developed style and possessed the self-confidence to coach the coach on the aesthetic dimension of coolness.

2. The contagion gap: Katie surprised me when she noted that Xers resent not being young anymore but feel bereft of adult options at the same time: "I'm twenty-eight and I still don't know what I want to do with my life." Meanwhile, her younger peers seem to feel ready to conquer the world, making it over in their image. Commenting on the sense of

rejection of Xers by Boomers, Katie concluded flatly, "We're not likeable."

3. The hipness gap: Janet and I grew up with television, and Josh and Katie are products of the computer age, but our Millennial friends are creatures of the Internet. Those three experiences are, of course, related, but the older the group the more commonly they feel technologically behind the times. For example, as Katie pointed out, "You guys [meaning Janet and I] had to tell us about MySpace." That's just not hip.

4. The uniqueness gap: with their numbers approaching eighty million and teenagers alone spending almost $130 billion annually, Millennials attract marketing attention the way the sun attracts planets,[14] widening the fissure between the generations. From Josh and Katie's perspective, the church (and culture in general) reaches out to the Millennials but overlooks the smaller Generation X because it's "so easy to get excited about the new person." Katie concluded wistfully, "We are still the stuck generation."

On one level, Josh and Katie's words represented a case study in how each dimension of cool also presents a way to lose it, meaning that uncool also takes many forms and expresses many subtleties sometimes difficult to put into words. These friends find themselves not so much behind technologically as culturally disenfranchised by the pressure they feel from a bigger, more confident Millennial tribe. The perception of declining value in the market of cool (although they still seem cool to us) symbolizes a journey that all leaders take eventually. The question is whether or not they can admit it.

Grace and Courage

The dark interior of the Kansas City steak house felt like the setting for a low-budget gangster film. I arrived for dinner carrying my almost-new smart phone (really a tiny computer that just happened to make calls) in a black vinyl case clipped to my belt. The case seemed like such a great idea: it freed my hands while carrying the phone, protected the device from harm, and kept it handy for calls. That is, until my friends Justin and Dan saw me carrying it that way and began laughing. They actually owned the identical device but would never dream of using the black plastic case that snapped shut. Their issue was not some flaw in the case design (it worked just fine) but the fact that using a case like this failed the cool test.

Hopes of reinvigorating my own cool by displaying the latest (at the time) phone technology seemed well founded at first. Only a few months earlier, hadn't I handed the box to an admiring Millennial who asked to look at the device so he could see it up close? But that was the phone itself. The presence of the case revealed my pathetic attempt to parlay a small box of electronics into a twenty-first-century identity. The reasons to hate the case seemed somewhat murky, but I sensed they arose from the pointlessness of protecting hardware rendered basically disposable by rapid technological change. Wearing the case at the beltline furnished even more entertainment for my friends, perhaps because of its association with the corporate casual style of dress popular among Boomers. Dan and Justin illustrated their point by citing an acquaintance who wore so many devices around his middle that they referred to him as sporting (like Batman) a "utility belt." Before our steaks arrived, I unclipped my case, removed the phone, and handed the case to my two mentors, part of the same group that had taught me to text message just a few years before. They accepted it as a token of surrender. Handing it over did not make me cool; it just presented a formal admission that I am not.

Saying "I am not cool" out loud hurts. If you don't believe me, try it right now. One reason very familiar to older leaders appeared in a blog by John Marshall, a sixth-generation minister, pastor of a large Baptist church, and friend: "I'm about to leave to go learn more at the conference for pastors under forty. I still feel nineteen, until I look in a mirror, and then I wonder who that guy is looking at me. I grew up in a world where the older always mentored the younger. The reverse seems to be happening these days."[15]

Admitting that my youth is behind me forms the first step in the process of acknowledging my lack of cool and blunts the pain of saying it the first time. Part of that pain issues from the fact that older leaders never received any preparation for the importance of cool as an issue or their inevitable decline in this market. Age and experience alone were supposed to guarantee a following, but it turns out that the beauty, hipness, uniqueness, and contagiousness we once assumed can be counted on no longer. Trying to bluff by dressing or acting differently only makes things worse.

Fortunately, a better option probably sits next to you at a meeting: a younger person or some other brand of unlikely friend who possesses both the knowledge you need and the willingness to share it. That person also needs the experience and wisdom you have to offer. It is not necessary to be cool or young to lead. It *is* necessary to have the grace to admit it when you are not.

2

CULTURE

"I Don't Get It"

Walking into a Starbucks in Middle America, Janet and I expected to leave in a few moments carrying not much more than a tall drip and a skinny latte. Choosing a table with nearby electrical outlets for our laptops, we started working. Some familiar faces appeared: Terry, Diane, and Erica had seen us the day before during a meeting with the young adult ministry of which they were members. Rounding up their own designer drinks, they joined us at the table and began debriefing the previous day's events. In just a week or so, Janet and I would be responsible for several presentations for a women's leadership forum on "Reaching the MySpace Generation," so we felt very fortunate to have primary sources sitting right in front of us in the form of these bright, likeable twentyish young women.

We began our interview by asking what life was like among their preadult female peers, a cohort sometimes referred to as "twixters" because of their social position between high school and the onset of full-time adult responsibilities. Previous conversations with young adults prepared us for some of what they said, but not for the way they summarized the predicament of young women: "We live in a circus." Specifically, they referenced manipulative tactics used to achieve power in their subculture: "If you know what to do and what to say, you can control anything," drawing particular attention to the mania for physical appearance as a method of control. These politically incorrect comments startled me but only introduced other subjects, such as their impression of how their peers experience preaching: "When you just tell me the Bible says 'don't do that' . . . it really doesn't connect. . . . It's awesome that the Bible says that . . . but so what?" They strongly believed that real change comes mainly through the influence of one person's life on another, not through morality lectures. The phrase "friends with benefits" character-ized their view of preadult female sexuality, with an emphasis on casual encounters, vague gender identity, and experimenta-tion: "Sexual tension has gotten a lot higher. . . . Even in middle school age they experiment with everything." Yet amid the many pressures of living in a circus, our new friends expressed the wish of their generation for mentors: "Always, always, always . . . there is that longing for an adult." From the midst of preadult chaos we heard a heart-wrenching plea for spiritual parenting.

These insights proved just as disquieting to those attending the women's leadership conference later that month, many of them mothers of young women living in the circus. The younger women present certified the authenticity of the conclusions we drew from the Starbucks interview. In less than an hour, Terry, Diane, and Erica gave us native insights into a culture we thought we understood quite well, helping us to see that in many important ways we did not get it at all. We had fallen into what my friend Jeffery, a regional youth minister, once referred to as *ethnoselfism*, the attractiveness of concentrating so hard on what matters to me that I miss evolving realities in the sur-rounding world. This chapter focuses on the use of a humbling admission about these realities ("I don't get it") and its ability to catalyze relationships with reverse mentors who put us in touch with the subcultures they understand.

Cultural Blackouts

When we recently moved back into the city from rural areas served only by broadcast television and dial-up Internet con-nections, we realized how little familiarity with media we actu-ally possessed. Hundreds of programming channels and the

experience of blazing broadband access to the Web, sampled in
hotels, suddenly appeared as regular features of our own lives.
We had some catching up to do. Our media drought put us out
of sync with some aspects of culture (such as watching music
videos from around the world), information (watching news
twenty-four hours a day), and entertainment (dozens of "Law
and Order" reruns every week). Although we were aware of the
broad outlines of events and trends, fine details often escaped
our notice. Similarly, leaders feeling very culture-current often
experience a blackout on certain subcultures of which they are
unaware. As one pastor put it, "Every day I get a little more disconnected unless I intentionally work at staying connected. We
live in a plug-and-play world, which poses a problem for many
of my peers who are hard-wired. They need what only the next
generation can give: connectedness."

Hard-wired leaders sometimes feel like the people who claim
to have been abducted by aliens from outer space, carried around
in a UFO for a while, and then returned to earth. Everything
looks familiar, but there are gaps in their memory and recogni-
tion. Former chief scientist for Xerox John Seely Brown captures
this predicament in a personal experience: "Recently, I was with
a young researcher . . . that had actually wired a web browser
into his eyeglasses. As he was having a conversation with me
he was actually bringing up my web page to read about me. This
was a bizarre experience, but except for watching his eye move-
ments, I was pretty much unaware that while he was talking to
me he was also reading about me."[1]

The shock of being Googled in real time might imply that
this encounter represents only an overly motivated graduate
student with too much hardware and too much time. But if we
think of culture as a particular vision of the world, and subcultures as subsidiary points of view, the browser eyeglasses are an
icon of a new way of seeing things, one that caught a scientist of
Brown's stature unaware—an experience most ministry leaders
my age know well.

These blackouts occur, in part, because of the way popular culture and the associated subcultural groups develop over time. In an interview, Anastasia Goodstein, a leading youth expert, describes the process as one of creating "space" (teen space, gamer space) for new forms of expression and ways of living. The inception of social networking sites such as Facebook illustrates how these spaces evolve. Beginning in the tech community, simple Web pages hosted at Internet locations such as GeoCities gave users a growing array of information to read, leading eventually to more interactive blogs (originally called "Web logs") that allowed readers to post comments on the writings and imagery supplied by an author. However, even blogs, from Goodstein's perspective, only replicated the offline world online, allowing electronic expression of many traditional forms of written communication. Social networking sites such as MySpace, though including blogging, began linking users together in multiple connections so vast as to offer an alternative to e-mail, the use of which is now declining. Merging video gaming technology with the networking ethos, virtual reality (VR) sites such as Second Life now allow users to become citizens and creators of whole new online worlds in which they function through avatars (three-dimensional, video gamelike characters).[2]

The evolutionary process that creates these new spaces generally begins with a small number of early adopters (often within an existing subculture), reaches a critical tipping point (sometimes impelled by a new technology), and then goes mainstream. So MySpace, one of the earliest and most popular social networking sites originally served to promote bands in the Los Angeles area, quickly developed into an international phenomenon. Danah Boyd, a scholar at the University of California at Berkeley who is working on developing the field of Internet anthropology, observes that in this progression *connectedness* trumps the human-computer interaction as the driving ethos of the Internet, "bringing together the estimated sixty million bloggers, those seventy-two million MySpace users, and millions more on single-use social networks where people share one category of stuff, like Flickr [photos], del.icio.us [links], Digg [news stories], Wikipedia [encyclopedia articles], and YouTube [video]."[3] To complicate matters, Boyd surmises that social networking site participants may now be generating their own subcultures as more conservative young people gravitate toward the relatively innocuous Facebook, while their less conservative peers concentrate on the edgier MySpace—for now.[4] The former site has the ethos of a university student union, while the latter features a dance club vibe. As with cool, the technologies that connect people also appear to offer the means for dividing them.

As a hard-wired leader, I find these cultural software updates simply falling outside my experiential grid. Moreover, the resources for understanding them certainly held no place in my ministry training. The consequent blackout easily develops into a deterrent from participating in mission to these subcultures, constituting an incentive to stay safely among our peers within the church and hoping that our marketing campaigns will somehow attract those unlike ourselves to join us. A reverse mentoring friendship offers an effective way not to join a subculture but to understand it from an insider's perspective such that it informs our mission to the subculture. Saying "I don't get it" out loud makes this friendship possible.

Janet and I encountered this kind of learning experience when we met twentysomething Zeke in a coffeehouse. In the course of his duties as the manager of this funky, downtown establishment, he stopped by our table to pick up some dishes and we began to chat. The motivation to ask the first question often defines the difference between an important learning opportunity and just another cup of coffee. We discovered that at night Zeke assumed another identity, as a musician in an alt-country band (a genre that he says fuses country music with an alternative rock vibe to create a new sound). Realizing that we had heard his band perform in a local venue, we started asking Zeke about culture, music, and spirituality.

What we heard reminded us of the "cultural creatives" that urban planner Richard Florida views as the crucial driving force behind the development of urban areas.[5] Ranging from software engineers to artists and musicians, this distributed nation creates much of the future we all live, from concentrations in places such as the San Francisco Bay Area; Madison, Wisconsin; and Austin, Texas. Zeke seemed to represent the "bohemian" type of creative. In response to our informal interview, he articulated some of the assumptions of his subculture on issues of life, art, and spirituality, issues that for him are connected in the most profound ways. If Zeke were to express these thoughts to main-streamers, they might sound something like this.

I Love Media, but I Trust My Friends

A lot of our conversation focused on music, a natural subject for Zeke. We compared notes on some bands, asking him what he liked. For example, he mentioned a group called Wilco, which I assumed to be alt-country until Erik, another R-mentor, instructed me that "technically they're not alt-country any-more. . . . I don't know how to categorize them . . . they kind of left alt-country seven or eight years ago." As Erik coached me to compare Wilco to mid-1970s soft rock (which predates his birth by a decade) or even the Beatles in their *Abbey Road* season, I felt good about being only seven years behind. Zeke then offered a one-item list of the music he found revolting: anything "mainstream." So I asked how he found out about the latest developments on the music scene. He mentioned Web-sites such as Pandora and MySpace but confessed simply that "I ask my friends." He finds the leading edge by relationship more than by research, a practice consistent with a survey of younger people finding that they assume important information natu-rally penetrates through the data that clutter their lives to reach them. So rather than relying solely on research, they trust that the information marketplace will deliver items of value to them automatically, often through relationship.

I Am Aware of Broadcasting, but I Trust Narrowcasting

We joked with Zeke about the importance of what our generation in its adolescence called "transistor radios." They brought us music that was portable and private enough to cordon off the rock-and-roll youth culture from our World War II–era parents. But we discovered that Zeke disdained radio, regarding it as pitifully trailing edge, more of a monument to what used to hold value than anything else. Moreover, he described its play lists as corrupt, overproduced, and fake. Zeke preferred the homegrown music available live in local clubs, online at obscure MySpace pages, or—best of all—the music you make yourself.

I Spend Money, but I Trust Art

We heard him imply that things done just for the money are not to be trusted. In fact, the worst slur on any form of music, from Zeke's perspective, is to label it "commercial." Authentic things rise up out of the pure joy of creation, and if the money follows that's fine. In fact, Zeke went so far as to say that although he embraces the hope that his band one day achieves prominence, he finds fulfillment in the joy of playing local gigs; the rest just takes care of itself at some point. Art merits trust for Zeke because, at least in the ideal, the creation exists for its own sake, offering a kind of purity that for bohemians parallels the concept of "holiness."

I Respect Excellence, but I Trust Authenticity

We discussed the trend among younger adults to prefer no one musical style, exhibited in iPods storing a thousand songs representing the best five selections by two hundred artists. Zeke laughed when we compared their anthology approach to the days when teenagers liked rock *or* folk, but not both. He pointed out that what defines the best music comes down to its honesty. A song truly reflecting an artist's convictions, talent, and personhood impressed Zeke much more than vocals and instrumentals washed through software to fit the needs of a mass marketing campaign. Authenticity, he felt, commands much greater respect among his peers than production values, no matter how impressive.

I Resist Church, but I Trust Jesus

To Zeke, the average Sunday morning worship service sounds just like radio: homogenized, overproduced, shallow, and obsolete. Though raised in a conservative denomination, he feels alienated from this kind of experience. Moreover, he expressed disappointment with his Christian customers—especially those from my fellowship, which he described as the most demanding and complaint-prone: "They walk around like they know something you don't know. But the way they are, I don't want to know what they know." Zeke finds Jesus compelling but shrinks from finding a spiritual home among his believing customers and the "radio" style of ministry to which they seem devoted. For Zeke, then, music serves as a metaphor for much else in life.

Yet we found his self-awareness refreshing. He accepts the fact that millions of people listen to the radio and that millions also attend conventional congregations, and he has no desire to inflict his preferences on them. His own authenticity and graciousness were not strategies to convert us into alt-country rockers but a genuinely friendly vantage point from which we gained insights into his subculture that no book offers. Clearly, neither traditional nor contemporary ministry forms held much appeal for Zeke or his peers. An alt-country guy and his friends require some kind of alt-church meeting them on their own terms. Zeke never said this to us directly in ending our blackout, but then he did not have to. The Zekes of the world respond well to anyone who will say "I don't get it," especially when the statement takes the form of asking questions.

Hard vs. Soft Reset

Feeling out of connection with important aspects of culture, combined with the seeming impossibility of ever getting caught up, poses a dilemma: How do leaders develop enough savvy to function effectively without totally deconstructing themselves in the process? I felt this sort of frustration for months when my first-generation smart phone (the one that came in the black case) simply refused to function as advertised. Constantly bogged-down software and nonfunctional e-mail only began the list of complaints in a technological tragedy that for me seemed to have taken on Shakespearean proportions. I called tech support and endlessly tried procedures in the manual, even jamming the stylus into a tiny hole on the side of the box to perform a "soft reset," all to no avail. My deliverance came in the form of a college-age man busily working a cell phone kiosk at a local mall who, out of his stream of consciousness multitasking, culled a few seconds to recommend something called a hard reset. The basic requirement of this procedure was courage. With all of the information on the smart phone temporarily erased in the process, the slightest failure meant tech suicide—techicide.

But it worked. In the process, a much younger mentor taught me by experience how to change things with a hard reset, something I had read about but feared. This experience clarified the plight of hard-wired leaders who often feel their only options are either to keep going as-is or attempt something like a hard reset, a radical and unprecedented change that could wipe out almost everything they value in the process. Because dramatically changing our approach to leadership is sometimes necessary, many leaders understandably hesitate to push the hard reset button. This kind of fear accounts for many conversations I've had in the last few years in which leaders admit to feeling unable, unwilling, or too old to change on this scale, especially when measured against the number of years left in their careers. I tell them I understand, because I do. My comprehensive knowledge of the mimeograph machine and the IBM Selectric II typewriter take up memory space in my brain that is now unavailable for reclamation and reuse. The instinctive response to this maldistribution of experience and memory is to shrink from the pain of a hard reset and thereby avoid any change or personal development at all. Even leaders who mean well and wish they understood culture better can fall under the gravitational pull of this kind of thinking, deciding by their inaction to remain blacked out.

An alternative exists in the form of what I would call a soft reset that does not erase our fundamental identity but definitely places a new perspective on how that identity is expressed in the way we do ministry and mission. I have found a master of this practice in interviewing thirty-five-year-old Andy Ford, who serves as chief insight officer for a Midwestern marketing firm. Among his other responsibilities, Ford specializes in helping large corporations who often try to "jam their product into someone's life" discover ways to "fit their product *around* people's busy lives."[6] The need for that discovery springs from the ease with which large organizations (and small ones) lose touch so easily with the very people they intend to serve. Spending millions on marketing research and consultants proves an inadequate remedy for this cultural blackout because leaders tend to focus on understanding products in almost infinite detail, to the exclusion of understanding customers beyond demographics and opinion surveys.

Resetting an organization's perspective may be soft, but it is hardly painless. Investigating communities frequented by trendsetting customers, Ford develops an informal rapport with them by "blending in [to] translate what's happening" in preparation for presentations to large companies, sometimes followed by full-scale culture immersion for their executives. The immersion puts these decision makers face-to-face with people who offer only a tepid response to conventional advertising. The encounters take place not in an office or a room equipped with a two-way mirror but on the customer's home turf, whether a bookstore, a skateboard shop, or a college campus searching for the authentic core of their experience. "Don't just cover it with a Cuban flag and call it Cuban," Ford quips. For one such trip, semipermanent tattoos applied to senior managers helped them become part of the activities of a local entertainment venue, allowing them to get close enough to the patrons to develop a feel for what they were like as people rather than just as consumers. Insight of this kind requires an almost visceral sensitivity to their culture and personalities, rather than a survey-based report on their traits and preferences (as valuable as such a report can be in other ways).

Whether presenting findings to a group of managers or taking them on a cultural excursion, Ford finds their comfort level often strained. "Much of what I say tends to affirm those who are looking forward," he notes, adding that he would be "shocked" to receive a unanimously positive response from his corporate audiences ("I would not be doing my job"). He has done his job so well with some companies that he has been met initially with skepticism and even "absolute disdain." Some of the response stems from his startling material, but some also is provoked by his youthful appearance, as if his much older audiences were saying to themselves, "Check out goatee boy." The field trips can prove even more challenging for some of Ford's clients, who frequently experience all the phases of culture shock in just a few hours but emerge with a new understanding of their potential markets and a new vocabulary for expressing those insights strategically. As Ford concludes, "If you don't speak the language, it doesn't matter how willing you are to learn." With the help of guides such as Ford, familiarity with the emotional language of a subculture allows even a huge enterprise to reposition itself for greater effectiveness in the market, often by creating a new product (for example, a handy stain-removing stick) that addresses an old need (doing the laundry).

He easily identifies the parallels to the kind of strategy some Christian leaders employ, involving a great deal of hard work that oddly never quite seems to gain traction in the community. "They're not coming," he observes, going on to state that necessary changes sometimes fall victim to the objection that "It's not biblical," another way of expressing fear of the hard reset and the perceived threatening abandonment of our convictions. Rather than a hard reset, we choose no reset at all and allow the gap between our ministry and our culture to widen by the hour. Ford's adventures in cultural immersion indicate that another path is open to leaders who are aware that they do not get it and are willing to turn to native sources of cultural insight.

Getting It

The influence of young mentors can show up everywhere in life and ministry. The way Janet and I thought of our last home, for example, changed significantly when a woman half our age advised us that a space in our basement served more naturally as a library than anything else. Her input, something we lacked the ability to see ourselves, radically altered how we used our home. In another instance, members of a local band, young enough to be our children, invited us to a downtown coffeehouse for an acoustic concert one weekend, placing us in an environment that grew into our second office over the next few years and serving as a window on the developing postmodern subcultures in our city. Janet's seminary coursework also benefited from the assistance of two younger women editors who offered correction with great gentleness. Their helpfulness stands as a symbol of what these unlikely friends offer. In healthy R-mentoring relationships, young tutors function not as the creators of our work or simply as critics but as our *editors*. The content we deliver means more and serves others better because we have known them.

Their influence also appears in other unlikely places. Generational consultant Marc Prensky cites the example of Microsoft, a dominating force in the computer industry of the 1990s but with virtually no cognizance of the Internet until young employees began bombarding Bill Gates with appeals to explore online business possibilities or risk the future of the company. Gates was so moved by their arguments that he issued a strategic change memo stating that, from now on, Microsoft's business would center on the Internet. In another instance of bottom-up transformation, American soldiers, finding their standard-issue equipment inadequate for field conditions in Afghanistan and Iraq, simply located better gear online and began ordering it on their own until their officers were won over.[7] Neither of these initiatives destroyed the enterprise involved, and both fostered a more responsive atmosphere and greater effectiveness by permitting the young to reverse the usual top-down pattern of decision making. The only requirement is someone at the top saying "I don't get it" but recognizing that someone else—and maybe not their first choice—does.

3

MINISTRY

"I Am Not Relevant"

The invitation to join a group of friends from church in Ruth's living room arrived unexpectedly. As the senior pastor of a largely young adult congregation in the Midwest, I knew that enjoying a meal together happened a lot, but not like this. Ruth, a staff pastor at our church, hosted the event, but the invitation came from our mutual friend Denise, who felt the need to confess some things to those closest to her.

Janet and I arrived at Ruth's suburban brick home to find about a dozen other friends and staff members gathered in the living room. The aroma of Denise's homemade enchiladas being warmed in the oven permeated the house. Everyone seemed happy to share an evening with everyone else, but no one knew exactly what to expect from this one.

After dinner, the small crowd began to settle into conversation in the living room, arranging themselves in a rough circle. As they assumed their positions, Denise took me aside to say that she had never confessed in front of a group before (that made two of us) and then asked for my pastoral wisdom for the moment. Having none, I bluffed, offering a commonsense recommendation to use discretion and keep it brief.

As we reentered the circle, conversation died down as she took her seat. In a few minutes of soft words and tears, Denise opened her life up to us, confessing, apologizing, and repenting in a way that was both honest and tactful. The group sat in complete silence until she finished her admissions and asked for our understanding and forgiveness. The silence lasted for a moment

until one friend spoke up, admitting that he and no doubt everyone else in the room struggled just as Denise did with life issues;
he went on to voice the love and forgiveness of the whole group.
At that point, a murmur of affirmation rose spontaneously from
around the circle, creating the opportunity for soft words and
tears, some of them my own. Our congregation's practices did
not include absolution, but I saw our members practice it that
evening anyway. Denise experienced forgiveness, healing, and
reconciliation, and the group grew in grace by extending it to
someone else.

My total contribution amounted to showing up, eating
enchiladas, and offering minimal advice. Denise fashioned the
whole event, with Ruth's logistical help, to take a chance on
confessing to her friends. As a pastor, I had never admired our
congregation more than I did that night. But driving home with
Janet, I began to wonder two things: First, if this kind of experience really grows people spiritually, why spend so much time
and money on running all the church machinery, the fruit of
which seems questionable? Second, in my many years of ministry, why does this experience stand alone as unique?

Denise's confession happened without my help. She had
found faith in Christ so recently as to actually believe that
the admonition found in James 5, to "confess your sins to each
other and pray for each other so that you may be healed,"[1]
deserved application simply because it appeared in the Bible.
Given enough time, she probably would have absorbed our habit
of abdicating that verse to Catholics in the confessional, or
mainliners reciting liturgies, or reframing it as merely a recommendation to apologize to those we wrong. In short, she was too
new to understand the highly nuanced perspective that afforded
"mature" Christians clever ways to evade the plain teaching of
the passage. Mystery solved: Denise's confession stood as unique
because I lacked the opportunity to teach her (by implication and example) that we Pentecostals just don't do that sort
of thing. So instead of waiting for a teacher, she unwittingly

stepped into the role herself and taught *me* what James meant and what honesty and forgiveness look like.

That night Denise served as my mentor, demonstrating grace by taking a huge risk, sacrificing pride for the sake of integrity. My presence lent only moral support to a courageous act that would have taken place anyway. In short, my title, position, and education all lacked relevance. This chapter deals with the power leaders can experience when they find the courage to say, "I am not relevant." Of course, because Jesus gave no expiration date for his commands to bring the gospel to the whole world or to love God and each other completely, every leader's importance persists for a lifetime—in one sense. But the principle of relevance and the practice of it are not necessarily identical. In principle, a pastor achieves significance through his or her calling and faithfulness; but in practice all of these attributes mean little if the people we hope to lead fail to respond predictably. Strategies admired for evoking the desired responses in one season (such as attendance, spiritual growth, and so on) easily become icons of what used to work in the next. Leaders unaware of this shift unwittingly earn the title of irrelevant.

Many key influencers in organizations find themselves at the limit of their abilities long before the midpoint of their career. Despite pure motives and hard work, their leadership models and skills simply clock out, not because they failed but because they succeeded in a world that no longer cares as much. Science fiction writer William Gibson opines that "the future has already arrived. It's just not evenly distributed yet."[2] Trained in an environment where the future's presence appears thin, leaders who encounter a denser concentration of it quickly find themselves wondering why their strategies, sometimes cloned from famously effective ministries, seem to hold little appeal to those searching for faith and offer little help to those attempting to grow it.

This crisis offers a great opportunity. The ability to say "I am not relevant" out loud forms one of the foundations for the discipline of reverse mentoring. This statement pertains to practical relevance, not the issue of whether the leader is called, or important to God, or valued by other people. But without practical relevance, the relevance in principle that comes from our calling begins to mock us, becoming a reminder of youthful dreams that have turned into middle-aged nightmares. Reverse mentoring connects older leaders with younger teachers, opening a path for enhancing the elder's practical relevance while the young draw from the wisdom and integrity of those who have been sustained by principle relevance for many years.

Relative Relevance

Searching for old software one day in my seminary office, I pulled a long-forgotten cardboard box out of a cabinet and found it packed with computer accessories. A small audience gathered as I sorted through the old gear, all of which had been in a state of suspended animation for somewhere between three and five years. The box contained a veritable Smithsonian exhibit of has-been hardware and software, a paper display case for the remains of a bygone age: the twentieth century. Along with a variety of lessons, I discovered:

- Two yellow mouse pads: once used in a national ministry promotion campaign. I had kept a second one as a backup. *Lesson:* beware of large media campaigns. This year's hot promotional item easily becomes next year's backup.
- Zip disks: a clumsy and expensive way of storing 5 percent of what my twenty-dollar flash drive now holds. *Lesson:* "beta" (the testing, tryout state of new technology) is now a permanent condition, so hold on to methods loosely because most of them are transitional, just preparation for the next thing.
- 1997 trip mapping software: my house at the time did not even exist in 1997. *Lesson:* the courage to admit that things have changed is the first step to changing things.

- Rubber bands: still as handy in the office as the day they shipped. *Lesson:* even when change is the oxygen of culture, I had better know what to hang on to.

These small examples speak to a larger concept: that practical relevance itself floats relative to the issues and the context involved. The expensive computer accessories and software that served as icons of what was called the "information age" in the 1990s were relegated to a cardboard box just a few years later, while the lowly rubber band continued its uninterrupted reign as an office necessity.

The challenge of maintaining relevance, then, defies easy explanation as simply an artifact of getting older. Eric, for example, a young church-planter friend facing a very formal meeting with a group of senior leaders, needed to appear in a suit and tie, something quite alien to his normal style. The suit represented no problem, but the necktie posed an issue: his native culture (Gen X) failed to supply the knowledge of how to tie one. So using the assets that his culture did furnish, such as turning the word Google into a verb, Eric searched several Websites that gave detailed instructions. Yet despite diligent practice, forming the correct knot proved beyond his ability, until a friendly Boomer, wise in the ways of the necktie, volunteered to tie it for him. In this setting, even the skills of the young prove irrelevant because, relative to the context, they represent something other than what produces results. The pressure comes from both directions. One young adult pastor from the Seattle area told me of a friend's lament that, when it comes to video games, "fourteen-year-olds are kicking our butt when we play online." This person's skills fail to pass the test of practical relevance when confronting a teenager rampaging through a game of *Halo 3*.

Collapsing the Practical into the Principle

One possible response to declining relevance is the insistence that my ministry forms offer something *better*, even as their fruitfulness erodes. Defining change in our context as negative, I see the unchanging nature of our strategy and practice serving as proof that we still represent the lofty values of the gospel message our society now sadly rejects. Although biblical values and the good news about Jesus are not in question here, many ministries struggle to embody them in congregation or community in a way people understand and care about. "Apathy Is the New Black" appears on the album cover of a hardcore band unwittingly commenting on this situation.[3] Many of our methods assume a ready market that stands willing to respond, if we simply supply awareness of what our churches and organizations offer. Corporations often spend millions of dollars only to discover that almost no one really cares about their product, even though they may use it occasionally. Much of the Christian church in the United States finds itself in the grip of the same phenomenon: people drop by occasionally, but an increasing share of the population searches for spirituality in other ways. Our methods no longer make sense to them.

Some leaders respond by digging in, fortifying their position by collapsing practical relevance into principle relevance. Larry, a widely experienced overseer of a denominational region, for example, has frequently observed the tendency of leaders to allow their practice of ministry to become their identity over time, meaning that their call to ministry becomes so intertwined with doing ministry in a certain mode that they lose the ability to see the difference. And so, to the pastor of a very traditional church, maintaining the look and feel of the traditions can seem almost as important as the reason these patterns exist. Among these leaders, Larry has also witnessed a communication style that treats dialogue as an exercise in restating one's views in a louder and louder voice. Although identifying these attributes with generations or cultures helps in understanding them, Larry's experience suggests the larger human proclivity for becoming what we do. Standing with my father in his office after preaching for him in a retirement service that capped forty years of pastoral ministry, I witnessed a man who lost more than a title. He lost himself. I also saw illustrated the temptation to treat any suggestion of the need for substantial change as an assault on that identity itself, sparking defensiveness and resistance. Feeling this pressure, leaders invent a new definition that identifies practical relevance completely with the faithfulness that characterizes principle relevance. As long as we persevere in the "truth," the rest will take care of itself.

Collapsing Principle into the Practical

A second response to the challenge of ministering to our communities takes the opposite form. Leaders willing to admit that they should be producing better or different results sometimes convert relevance into just another tool. Witnessing this process multiple times in site visits around the country, I've observed that it often functions by simply "hot syncing" what bloggers would call the ministry's look and feel with the surrounding culture, as if plugging a PDA into a laptop to harmonize the databases on both. Doug, for instance, met me in an airport on his way to interview with a church interested in creating a high-impact program for young adults. His mix of gifts fit the project well, and his experience with ministry to this age group (his own) stretched back a couple of years. The challenge lay on the other end. The host church leadership had simply visited a prominent ministry of this kind, decided to copy the model, developed a large budget to finance it, and sought a magnetic young leader to make it fly. The approach revolved a lot around a dedicated space, elaborate coffee bar, minimalist furniture, and many, many flat screen plasma TVs. Hot sync: Starbucks meets IKEA meets nightclub meets NASA. Doug wanted nothing to do with it because he felt the church's brand of "relevance" held the potential for attracting people—but mainly Christians looking for a cooler worship venue. When used this way, relevance inadvertently becomes an *end* and not a means, creating a ministry with a cutting-edge appearance but whose primary focus is not on reaching out. The blank looks I get when asking staff members of such ministries about the percentage of their attendance drawn from the community rather than from other churches tell the story.

Another young adult leader facing the same challenge in a different part of the country told me that the people in his ministry change so rapidly and turn over so often that chasing their trends in order to adapt almost guarantees failure. Instead, he changes the ministry itself every ninety days or so, holding the interest of the young adults through the use of strategic uncertainty, motivating *them* to chase him. In other words, they will show up and bring "unchurched" guests because they *don't* know what will happen. However, in my field studies this sort of example seldom appears. More frequently, I encounter a pastor, old or young, whose complaint goes something like this: "I don't understand it . . . we got rid of the suits and ties on Sunday morning, our music is really contemporary now, and we use videos that look just like YouTube to do the announcements . . . and it's still not working!" What this exasperated person means is that they thought becoming meaningful in their community was as simple as a change of style, a type of cosmetic surgery for ministry. University ministry strategist Curt Harlow refers to this trait as "groomification," the notion that the way to appeal to young adults is to "change the 'cool' factor of your ministry. By dressing up the Dockers-loving pastor in an übercool Abercrombie & Fitch shirt with a matching American Eagle belt buckle. . . . Please believe me when I say that young people are not leaving because the leaders are not hip. Sometimes, in fact, our efforts to be trendy drive them away."[4] Our issues, then, are far more than cosmetic.

My friend Steve, a church planter in the northwest, describes this approach as hoping for success by switching to an "untucked" model of ministry, the power of which supposedly derives from appearing in worship services with shirt tails out.

This model often brings with it better haircuts and installation of an espresso bar in the lobby. All of these steps are commendable in their place, unless they become a substitute for the kind of transformation that attunes us to Jesus' mission in the world. Lacking this kind of change, we end up preaching or leading the same group of (more caffeinated) believers—usually assembled by transfer from other churches—but in an untucked shirt. Our neckties are safely at home, but so are virtually all of those outside of the faith in our community. Even if the edgy appearance of our ministry escapes irrelevance in the short run, "Who is to say," remarks one young pastor, "that in ten years coffee shops and small groups will not fall into the same category?"

Relevance Styles

The pain of declining practical relevance jolts Christian leaders. Although our calling comes from God, our influence flows from "being examples to the flock."[5] When we feel that others no longer find our example compelling, or our ministries significant, we sense our influence slipping away, and with it sometimes our faith. Despair can be the result. This struggle is hardly confined to vocational ministry. Even pop music icon Billy Joel, deciding to hand off the lead vocals on one of his compositions to another singer, commented, "I knew I wasn't the person to sing it. . . . I've already had my day in the sun—and to be honest, I'm not a big fan of my own voice."[6] In private conversations, I have heard more than one leader admit an almost paralyzing level of *obsolescence anxiety*, feeling their "day in the sun" passed so long ago that their potential in a complicated new world now approached zero. In the words of one parachurch leader, this feeling can begin as a rhythmic whisper that sounds like, "I used to know. I used to know. I used to know." Later it reaches a crescendo that drowns out the voice of hope in some leaders while driving others into defensiveness.

Freedom from defensiveness and despair involves many things, but none more important than reframing relevance—not just as theological principle or pragmatic tool but as a kind of *style* that leaders adjust over time by capitalizing on the relative nature of the concept itself. In other words, even when bereft of power over my situation, I still hold the power to make choices about how I *act* in that situation. These choices offer an opening for greater fruitfulness in the future for leaders who find the grace to say out loud "I am not relevant," or "I am not as relevant as someone else could be," as an invitation to reverse mentoring.

I found an example of this particular grace in operation while visiting a Christian radio station for a live interview about my then just-released book *Off-Road Disciplines*. During commercial breaks in the studio, I asked the program's hosts, John and Jennifer (he in his early thirties and she in her twenties), about the art of doing good radio. They advised me to speak as if to one individual because radio is a personal medium, and to imagine that person as an almost-forty female. Going live again with their questions, I proved incapable of putting their counsel into practice. My answers sounded as if they were addressed to an auditorium full of middle-aged men. Ironically, even answering questions on reverse mentoring in the presence of two young tutors did not improve my performance. Apparently, altering our "default" approach to things, although certainly possible, seldom yields to just one attempt at change.

However, a more profound lesson awaited me in the small lobby just outside the studio. I expected my friend Bob, the station manager, to conduct the interview as the long-time host of the morning show. In consultation with the station's owners, Bob arrived at the conclusion that younger voices were needed during drive time. The change resulted not from any lack of professionalism in Bob's performance but from his honest realization that possessing "experience" carried with it a demographic penalty—his life phase no longer paralleled that of the station's desired audience closely enough to be sure of an intuitive connection. He held citizenship in another world, one in which there were no twenty-five-year-old citizens. In truth, Bob's professionalism probably assured him a role as morning host for a lot longer, but he valued the station's effectiveness over entitlement and handed over the reins to John and Jennifer for an unprecedented experiment with young talent.

Bob simply found a new way to be relevant. Vacating the host's chair on the station's flagship morning program after twenty years of experience gave younger talent a chance to discover their potential. Bob's shift to afternoon radio represented "a step back professionally," but it also represented a step up strategically, allowing him to focus more on big-picture issues involved in operating the station and developing its future.

Another friend, now serving as a missionary in Europe, shared with me the same pain of surrendering his frontline role among younger adults. "I used to be that guy," he said, referring to his shift to managing missionary endeavors from behind the scenes. Clearly, this kind of work represented something other than what he expected at this life stage. But he, and Bob, bravely took a step back in order to take a step up in influence, beginning to contribute in a whole new way on the strategic level. Both were willing to surrender their definition of relevance for greater "revelance," the power of a ministry to embody and reveal the person of Christ in its community.

While thinking through the issue of relevance styles, I noticed a television documentary oddly titled, "How William Shatner Changed the World." The program, narrated by its namesake, depicts many technological advancements supposedly inspired or at least predicted by the *Star Trek* television series of the 1960s and its successors.[7] Although quite entertaining, this quasi-documentary also held symbolic importance for me on the issue of relevance. Starting his acting career in the days of black-and-white television, Shatner made his mark as a young leading man, a skill he capitalized on in playing his signature role as

Captain Kirk. Rather than surrender to midlife, he donned a hairpiece and found a new niche in the police drama *TJ Hooker*. Involved in a variety of lesser-known projects, he reemerged as a senior citizen to star as a quirky attorney in *Boston Legal*, almost a parody of his original black-and-white roles. He may not have saved the world, but he certainly saved himself from irrelevance. Leaders enjoy the same option provided they can recognize the natural disconnection of their ministry from culture, inviting unlikely people into their lives as guides to relevance in new forms.

No Defense

Every leader is relevant if she or he can define the appropriate relevance style. Several years ago, I faced a choice between styles when deciding to leave our third pastorate to direct doctoral studies for my denomination's seminary. Making the decision involved weeks of personal struggle, but the potential of exerting some measure of influence over a generation of future leaders simply proved irresistible. I was not disappointed, but I write this chapter having resigned from the seminary to plant a new congregation in Berkeley, California, with Janet. The seminary season was a positive experience, but in contemplating the possibility of becoming a church planter at this stage of life I needed a very good reason.

From almost the first day of our decision-making journey, I asked Byron Klaus, the seminary's president, to help us walk through the process. He offered coaching, friendship, wisdom, and prayers. As closure approached on the decision, he counseled me one day with words like these: "A time comes when you have to put the things you have taught into concrete terms." In my Pentecostal fellowship, we often perform the concrete first and then join institutions of higher education to teach about it later. I seemed to contradict this pattern by considering the unthinkable: trading in the ivory tower for the very concrete world of church planting in a post-Christian context.

Under the surface, though, the prospect of an adventure like this had been percolating up for quite some time. It took shape initially during a pancake breakfast with the Southern Baptist Convention's missionary strategist, Ed Stetzer. Talking through some of the issues we shared in higher education, I mentioned that something stirred inside me when I thought about leading a congregation again, but that I felt little pull toward most conventional ministry forms. "Why don't you plant a church?" he asked as casually as inquiring about the model of car I drive. I swallowed hard and began a litany of well-practiced reasons, including age, busyness, lack of experience, and a distaste for poverty, all of which I liked to refer to as "wisdom." He shrugged them all off and encouraged me to get involved anyway. I found the fact that Ed had done this himself to be both unfair and unnerving, but the challenge simply never went away. Eventually, in a blog I confessed to the world that basically only one thing stood between me and starting a new church: fear. The gradual solidification of our call meant that the potential of ministry in Berkeley began to feel larger than the fear of all the ways in which exploring it could go wrong. Ultimately, when the moment of decision came, Janet rendered the verdict by saying simply, "We have no defense against this."

Hopefully, our church planting initiative represents a new relevance style for the autumn of our ministry, bringing real-time ministry experience into the classroom and sending young leaders to the world. By facilitating this kind of ministry, we hope to finish the race more relevant rather than less. Leaders who share this ambition need to summon the courage to say some form of "I am not relevant," which might be "I am not as relevant here as I could be somewhere else." This admission sends all of us in search of ways to strengthen our grip on principle relevance and locate the resources for reinventing our practical relevance.

Part Two

CULTIVATING SPIRITUALITY

4

VISION

Seeing Beyond Ourselves

Allen tapped me on the shoulder as I dropped into a theater seat in the first row of the auditorium. The group of pastors who had just heard my presentation on cultural trends had seemed intrigued by my mention of a new area of research. During my trip from the airport to the hotel prior to the event, I found the rental car's radio already tuned to a hip-hop station. Having grown up in a middle-class, Anglo suburb when rock and roll was still new, I had to admit to knowing very little about this cultural juggernaut. Yet the music that flooded the interior of the rental car somehow ignited my curiosity and held it, as I formed a silent decision to pursue hip-hop as my next research interest. I had suspected that it held many times the impact of academic postmodernism but understood it so little that conclusions escaped me. "I just don't get it" summarized the impressions of hip-hop that introduced my talk on the effects of postmodernism in emerging culture.

Allen leaned over the back of my chair and said, "You do get it . . . you just don't know that you get it." He offered to spend some time with me during a break to explain how my overview of postmodernity[1] tied into hip-hop culture. Talking later in the Starbucks-esque coffee lounge around the corner, I discovered that Allen held a Ph.D. in educational leadership and was pastoring an inner-city church he had founded. Patiently, he walked me through the ways in which hip-hop, starting as an

African American cultural expression, developed into a global force. He described it as a "post-civil-rights" musical expression and detailed the tension within the African American community over its merits and impact. Allen described much of his community in general terms as divided among Motown, doo wop, soul/R&B, and hip-hop roughly along generational lines. The latter he described as "confrontational" in a way that sometimes made the other generations nervous and judgmental. In fact, Allen taught a seminary class on the history and theology of the African American Church. During one class he brought in a panel of hip-hop-generation young adults to interact with the students. Asked why they did not attend church, several responded pointedly, "We are not accepted at church."

I enjoy this kind of interview tremendously and took notes on my PDA as fast as my thumbs would move until Allen gave me the gift of the truth with a simple question: "Are you aware that all the faces on your slides are white?" I was quiet for a moment, mentally reviewing my PowerPoint presentation in hopes of finding exceptions other than one graphic of Oprah Winfrey, included because she was famous, not because she was black. All I could say was, "Thank you." It had never occurred to me that my presentation on cultural diversity involved a painful irony: the slides featured all Anglos plus Oprah—a white person's view of the world. I wanted to blame the embarrassing gaffe on the fact that the discussion of postmodernism in the church seems to be mainly a preoccupation of whites. But the blindness was in fact my own.

In Allen's case, his cultural tutoring was "reverse" not just because he was younger (although he was) but because our encounter was unlikely and cut across cultures. This chapter outlines how leadership makes us blind to the very realities we need to engage; it presents the case for R-mentoring as one means to restore the kind of vision that enables leaders to see the potential of both the present and the future in new ways.

Positional Blindness

Jesus responded to criticism from the Pharisees by referring to them individually as "blind guides" and then describing the effect of their spiritual leadership in Israel in even harsher terms: "If a blind man leads a blind man, both will fall into a pit."[2] A modern organizational consultant might have defined their problem as simple lack of flexibility, but Jesus traced it to something deeper, to their love of having the best seats in the synagogue and at public banquets, and the way they relished being called "Rabbi" in the marketplace.[3] Their devotion to the position of spiritual leadership exceeded their devotion to what that role represented in their ancient nation. Position became a ticket to status, and status rapidly clouds the vision of the very best of us. To the blind eye, even a sequence of all-white faces can appear multicultural.

By simple virtue of holding a leadership role, then, we become susceptible to the same forces that isolated the Pharisees from reality, what organizational theorists refer to as "skilled incompetence," the trait of high-functioning people who find clever ways to evade learnings that might challenge their role or function too drastically.[4] Even some successful reverse mentoring initiatives in the corporate world have run into resistance that was due to the reluctance of senior leaders to embrace the need for new skills, or their reluctance to adopt technologies (that is, anything with a keyboard) that seemed more naturally the province of support staff. One top General Motors executive compared the feeling to "watching other people do dives from the high diving board. . . . Suddenly it's my turn—and I'm not getting out of this one."[5] The higher the position, the farther the drop to the water, and the more sensible it seems to use power to avoid jumping.

The temptation to allow position to obscure perspective does not make those in leadership roles worse than anyone else; it's just that they are *like* everyone else despite being called "the leader." Harry, for example, told me of asking a homeless man living on the streets of a large urban area, "What would you be if you could be anything at all?" The man gave a one-word reply: "Visible." This word is now expressed in Harry's career in urban photography, creating stunning, large-scale black-and-white imagery designed to make the homeless visible to others.

Similarly, leaders who do not take deliberate steps to keep others visible will find a conspiracy of circumstances, such as lack of time and the occupational hazard of talking instead of listening, gradually diminishing their perceptual acuity. In one R-mentoring initiative among lawyers, for example, simple factors such as these kept the benefits of advanced technology from being applied to the practice of law by almost a decade.[6] Jennifer Deal's multiyear survey of employees finds intergenerational conflict in the workplace rooted less in cultural mysteries than in an old-fashioned struggle over "clout" between those who have it and those who want it.[7] This dynamic alone means that potential reverse mentors may remain naturally divided from those they could help unless everyone involved does something about it.

Positional blindness, then, may sound like an organizational issue (which it becomes), but the condition develops and is sustained one decision at a time. One of my decision points arrived unexpectedly while sitting with two youth ministers in an office that looked as if it had been designed by IKEA. I could hear the conference to which they had invited me taking place in another part of the building as we reflected on the talk I had just given in particular, and on youth culture in general. Their insights were startling, revealing that my assumptions about communicating with teens were exactly backward in some ways. For example, they tutored me on aiming presentations at the older students because the younger ones will follow along, exposing my opposite assumption as completely wrong. I shook my head in surprise.

My teachers continued to offer friendly, insightful, and gracious counsel. But when the conversation turned to *my* presentation specifically, I felt a sudden spike of anxiety, knowing that I was about to receive personal feedback from two experts in communicating to this age group. I silently weighed the certain benefits of their wisdom versus the potential pain, but the internal conflict embarrassed me. Having championed reverse mentoring around the country, I found myself unable to practice it in front of two leaders young enough to be my sons. After all, I was a plenary speaker and had the brochure to prove it. My repentance took the form of asking them how to become more effective in communicating with teens, during which I felt like a blindfolded prisoner waiting for a firing squad—only to find myself struck by encouragement rather than bullets.

The vision that was needed to see the potential benefits of this relationship came not from my own plans or research but from an unspoken act of repentance that gave these young tutors permission to speak into my life in a tangible way. The point is not so much the nature of their advice as the discipline of submitting to unlikely teachers and the new perspective they opened up for me by virtue of our differences, not our similarities. Regularly stretching across cultural lines to learn can help to restore the vision of leaders of all ages and cultures.

Personal Blindness

Position obscures our vision because leadership roles by definition tend to be isolating, eroding such assets as time and relationship while substituting temptations such as pride and preoccupation. Both disconnect us from a constantly morphing world. One of the challenges presented by that world, according to the influential researcher and consultant Don Tapscott, is that "for the first time in history, kids are more important to innovation than their parents."[8] The impact of this reality is felt everywhere in our society, but perhaps most acutely in popular culture and technology, two forces that are becoming increasingly intertwined. Firms such as Google and countless dot coms, founded by the young, are now icons of the dominant and some-times unnerving role the young play in creating the future where we will all live.

The same force is alive and well in ministry leadership. My field research for the last several years has turned up an unmis-takable and understandable correlation between youth (and young thinking) and the development of new approaches to ministry, with the most prominent examples occurring in church planting. Rather than following the conventional pattern of implementing a system of small groups after starting up services, my friend Ted, for instance, started house churches and then developed a large group worship meeting from them. When I expressed a desire to learn more from his ministry by visiting, he responded, "I don't know what to tell you . . . we just hang out." An older (or older-thinking) leader raised and trained where the atmosphere of the future was thinner might be unable to discern this opportunity or act on it without Ted's help.

Filters

Having influence later in life is supposed to be one of the things that makes aging worth it. My generation has arrived at its lead-ership prime only to find that younger people, though perhaps serving under us on the flowchart, can eclipse us in creative con-tribution, cultural insight, and (worst of all) cool. Formed in the burgeoning youth culture of the 1960s, Boomers find the irony almost painful to behold. Even with the best of intentions, and apart from the influences of power, some fail to perceive what is plainly going on around them, cultivating an organizational opaqueness in which leadership is actually unaware that its point of view does not represent reality. In the same way that holding my hand in front of my face can block out an object the size of the moon in the night sky, the assumptions native to my culture (its filters) can stand in the way of seeing large realities in my path. The first casualty can be the ability to detect the subtleties so crucial to any other culture. While attending a young adult congregation, for instance, I was taken aback to realize that the hundred or so college-age people who appeared simply "young" to me actually saw each other in terms of clear-cut tribal groups (Geeks, Jocks, Nerds, Rockers, etc.), subcultures that sometimes had trouble connecting with each other. I could see them, but my more homogeneous cultural background obscured many of the differences among them. We tend to see "culture" everywhere except in the mirror.

Ministries and other organizations share the same sort of concern. In the mid-1990s, for example, General Electric was largely out of sync with the potential of Internet-based business models. Without the direct intervention of CEO Jack Welch mandating a reverse mentoring program for his executives, this lack of vision might have been GE's undoing in the twenty-first century, not because the corporation's leadership was unaware of the Internet or lacked the motivation to succeed but because its perspective on the Internet was not clear enough to discern the need for exploring new ways of doing business. Simply put, a sixty-year-old executive who did not even own a PDA very likely lacked the personal history and cultural insight to perceive where the Web was taking business and everything else. The crucial skill here is not technical expertise but the ability to recognize this blindness and then use reverse mentors to help you develop a new form of vision.

Much of the change management field has arisen out of the need to address the struggle of intelligent, well-meaning people striving to make sense out of what is happening around them and to define a viable future. When individuals gather to create an organization, the inevitable outcome is creation of a collective "box" (the one we all seem to want to get out of) that, as with all cultures, brings along forms of vision and forms of blindness. In a conversation over dinner, for example, a Norwegian scholar told me of his observation that Goths (young people emulating the style and culture of the gothic rock scene of the early 1980s) who join Christian churches in his country tend to retain the attributes of their subculture (black clothing and dramatic makeup) while their peers outside the faith leave them behind as they age. Assimilation into a faith community seems to freeze these young adults in a Goth look, at least for a season, while friends move on with their lives. Becoming an insider, then, changes how we interact with those on the outside, sometimes depriving us of the lessons they have to teach.

Jealousy

The sensation of slipping toward permanent residence at the trailing edge fosters strong reactions among those who feel they deserve to be pacesetters. Trend analyst Anastasia Goodstein, for example, has observed older leaders articulating "negative stereotypes" about the young. She points out, of course, that these cohorts do have very distinct views on specific issues, such as how much of one's life it is appropriate to make public on the Internet, or why a nineteen-year-old would send an instant message rather than talk face-to-face to someone in the next office.[9] But these disparities, although daunting, don't seem sufficient to explain some of the disdain for the young that I have witnessed among my peers as well. Perhaps a spiritual issue simmers under the surface: jealousy.

Considering this possibility, it is difficult to evade the parallel to King Saul hurling a spear twice at the faithful but younger and more popular David, an attack he would repeat when his own son Jonathan interceded on David's behalf. The fact that Saul was prophesying accompanied by David playing the harp "as he usually did" did not stop the king from reaching for his weapon. Such is the power of the "jealous eye" he kept on the young war hero who received public adulation from Israel on a level the King could never hope to match. "What more can you get but the Kingdom?" was the question that haunted Saul, along with "an evil spirit from God," perhaps provoked by the same bondage to envy.[10] Christian leaders who fall victim to this attitude toward cooler, more culture-current, more talented young people also reach for spears. Their weapons may take the form of critical words, passive withholding of the resources the young need to flourish, or the outright firings that I have witnessed in churches. David dodged these spears. I can only hope that my younger friends have the same grace, and that unlike David they will not fall into similar sins later in life.

In *The Four Loves*, C. S. Lewis identifies this jealousy as surging up within us when someone we think of as part of our group "flashes ahead," leaving the others in a static position while the innovator is "flooded with new interest" of some kind, sparking the question, "Why was it never opened to us?"[11] The struggle to answer this question often results in a dismissive attitude toward those we envy, accompanied by ridicule or the assertion that their interests or abilities are really nothing new (a claim I have heard often about young-thinking ministries). Lewis confesses candidly that his own profession of university teacher carried the obligation to resist this temptation: "If we are any good we must always be working towards the moment at which our pupils are fit to become our critics and rivals. We should be delighted when it arrives, as the fencing master is delighted when his pupil can pink and disarm him. And many are."

I have never experienced a single minute of training in how to be "disarmed" by those who are supposed to be my followers. Understandably, anxiety about being surpassed by the younger and cooler (or by anyone for that matter) then creates pressure to distance ourselves from them, just as the rewards of our relationship are about to accrue. Lewis tells the story of the university professor "Dr. Quartz" to illustrate the problem:

> No university boasted a more effective or devoted teacher. He
> spent the whole of himself on his pupils. He made an indelible

impression on nearly all of them. He was the object of much well merited hero-worship. Naturally, and delightfully, they continued to visit him after the tutorial relation had ended— went round to his house of an evening and had famous discussions. But the curious thing is that this never lasted. Sooner or later—it might be within a few months or even a few weeks— came the fatal evening when they knocked on his door and were told that the Doctor was engaged. After that he would always be engaged. They were banished from him forever. This was because, at their last meeting, they had rebelled. They had asserted their independence—differed from the master and supported their own view, perhaps not without success. Faced with that very independence which he had labored to produce and which it was his duty to produce if he could, Dr. Quartz could not bear it. . . . Dr. Quartz was an unhappy man.

Unhappy people make mistakes, and chief among them in the business context is allowing quiet envy to twist the opportunity for partnership with the young into a sad parody.

Asking a younger person for instruction exposes the deception from which jealousy gains its power: the notion that everything gained by them must somehow be a loss to me. This subtle fraud treats leadership as an earned status that entitles me to certain privileges, rather than a calling imparted by grace that means surrendering my own preferences for the sake of others and rejoicing in their success. Confessing my lack of understanding to a younger person and expressing willingness to take his or her counsel seriously brings a healing grace back into the relationship. Without fail in these situations, I have found that the younger person's esteem for the older actually increases when help is requested, spinning off two paradoxes: (1) the younger person eventually requests to be mentored by the older as well; and (2) the older leader becomes not just more effective but more content and comfortable with this season of life. Dr. Quartz had it wrong.

New Lenses, Classic Frames

The best part of every conference happens in the lobbies and hallways, where relationships are nurtured. During an event on the West Coast, I sat in a large church entryway with Art and Danielle, career missionaries who mentor us on missiology among other things. As we sipped coffee, twentysomething Sandra walked up and introduced herself. She had read in the conference literature that we shared a common denominational heritage. Immediately I noticed her glasses, light pink plastic frames, studded with rhinestones, and pointy at the corners. When I said, "I like your glasses, Sandra," she replied, "They were my grandmother's; I just had new lenses put in them." Overcoming the visual impairments that can afflict older leaders does not mean throwing away our glasses, but instead putting new lenses into classic frames.

Turning to another subject, I discovered that she was a technical writer and asked, "So, Sandra, what's the secret of great technical writing?" Anyone brilliant enough to create clear and concise computer software manuals definitely had skills from which I could learn. But her response was unanticipated: "I write it so my mother could understand it." The implication of her reply turned some things upside down: her grandmother's look is the new standard of "cool," while her Boomer mom's computer knowledge is the new standard of obsolescence. She merges these realities by treasuring a memento of her grandmother's time, and with appropriate lenses installed she writes software manuals her mother could use.

Accepting that the unlikely might have new lenses through which to see the world is not easy. Facilitating a group discussion among theology professors gathered for a seminar, I found them full of creative ideas to pass along to the event's organizers, until we came to the issue of involving students in our discussion of ministry training in higher education. Suddenly the rapidity of their contributions to our very energetic discussion slowed and the clarity of their ideas spiraled downward into ambivalence, plainly communicating reluctance to see their profession through the eyes of its consumers—the students. Mild defensiveness of this kind is understandable among professional educators who generally have not been in school themselves for years, sometimes decades. But all ministry leaders face the challenge of closing their eyes to the world they are called to reach because their position, their person, or both, makes it easy to do so. In the for-profit context, one consultant expressed his frustration this way: "You don't have to spend half a million dollars on research. Just go and observe . . . go out and talk to customers to find out what they want."[12] Ministry leaders are not trying to discover customer preferences, but they do need new lenses to correct the natural decline of their vision.

5

WISDOM

Knowing Beyond Our Information

I had almost forgotten the pale green, four-drawer filing cabinet that sat for years in the basement of the seminary. Crammed with old sermon notes, research files, retreat presentations, and other ancient things, the cabinet had become the unofficial archive for two decades of my pastoral and parachurch ministry. Then the school requested that the basement be purged to make room for things that were needed. Because I had not looked at the files in the green cabinet for at least five years, they certainly seemed to fit the archive definition, so a teammate and I loaded cardboard boxes with hanging folders accessorized with the plastic tabs designed to order my entire universe alphabetically. Their final resting place would be the yellow dumpster in the parking lot behind the school.

Going through the folders, I watched my life pass before my eyes like the proverbial drowning person. Here is the program for the couples retreat Janet and I presented in New England twenty years ago; there are the sermons on Genesis written by somebody who used to be famous; and there sits my teaching series on the book of Revelation, once available on a break-through media known as audio cassette. We put the boxes on a black steel cart, fittingly the kind originally designed to roll overhead projectors through school hallways, and trundled them into an elevator, out into the parking lot, and right up to the dumpster. Unlocking the security padlock, I flung the big plastic lid backwards on its hinge and heaved the first box of files up over the rusty rim, watching the green and buff folders avalanche down into the smelly pit below. With them, a certain kind of life slid over an event horizon into history, a place in the past from which recovery is impossible—a small funeral for the information age. Each of those files seemed so precious at the time, because, as a pastor or teacher, I could need any one of them at any moment. But in fact, had the green filing cabinet in the basement been stolen, I would not have been able to tell the police what it contained other than "files." The storage media was its most salient feature, with the contents serving only as a growth medium for mold, all of it the product of my affinity for information.

One trend-tracking Website refers to this malady as "infolust," a trait driven by the basic human need to control the environment around us coupled with the assumption that information offers that kind of control.[1] If there were a recovery group for this affliction (Information Anonymous), I would have to introduce myself by saying, "My name is Earl . . . and I'm an information addict." Like some other addictions, this one cultivates a powerful ability to rationalize: Wasn't more information better than less? Wasn't information power? Wasn't a teacher supposed to supply information to students? But also like other addictions, recovery requires a big dose of the truth.

This chapter makes the case that for leaders wisdom should be prioritized above information, and that reverse mentoring is one of the disciplines crucial to being wise. The alternative is a kind of info-syncretism in which the pursuit of data becomes more important than the purpose for which we are collecting them.

Information

The half-ounce plastic flash drive in my pocket holds astronomically more digital data than existed on earth fifty years ago. But part of me grows increasingly suspicious about whether volume storage like this is a universal benefit to ministry. This issue ripened as I made the transition from seminary professor to church planter. I gave away most of the books I could have borrowed for free from the library but instead bought on Amazon to line the tall oak bookshelves in my office. The pile that I took with me was much smaller than the heap I left on a countertop in the student lounge to feed the habit of other addicts. A positive sign of recovery, though, emerged from the strange sense of relief I felt, not from acquiring more information but from divesting myself of it.

My growing doubts about the value of accumulating data stem from a commonsense market reality: as quantity grows, price declines. Imagine what diamonds would cost, for example, if they were as available as 9-volt batteries. So much text, graphic, and video material (to name just three genres) is being generated every few seconds that the perceived value of any one piece of data simply must soften. That's why we feel the need to acquire more, to feel "informed." Nonetheless, the impossibility of keeping up grows more disheartening every day. Consider these indicators:

- The average American already spends 146 days out of every year consuming media.
- Having started in obscurity, YouTube now pumps 27 petabytes (that's 27 million gigabytes) of user-generated video into our computer screens monthly.
- A simple search for "leadership" books on Amazon generates almost 250,000 hits, and counting.[2]

Leaders help to drive this market reality because we operate under the assumption that mastery of certain subjects or sources will lead to better decisions based on comprehensive knowledge. The logic of this premise is supported by countless anecdotes of good information leading to improved decisions. But this outcome is hardly universal.

After years of supplying survey research to church leaders for this reason, George Barna resigned himself to the limits of knowledge with these words: "The strategy was flawed because it had an assumption. The assumption was that the people in leadership are actually leaders. [I thought] all I need to do is give them the right information and they can draw the right conclusions. . . . Most people who are in positions of leadership in local churches aren't leaders. They're great people, but they're not really leaders."[3]

America's leading researcher on marketing the church is suggesting that the problem is not in our data but in us. With these dynamics in place, it seems unlikely that sole reliance on *more* information is a viable future for leaders needing to make critical decisions for their ministries.

Yet as a member of the television generation, I sometimes still think of the Internet as an "information superhighway," a very fast electronic postal service or library that can feed my longing for data. My reverse mentors, native to the Internet, laugh at me. They have assisted my recovery by helping me grasp *different* ways of handling the millions of words and images that flood my inbox, hard drive, and shelves. They showed me that all these "facts" can just as easily imprison my thinking as liberate it. This counsel seemed backward to a modern like me, raised on the certain-as-gravity assumption that knowing more was the primary driver of all human progress. When in doubt, I did research.

The smirks on the faces of my R-mentors when seeing my paper files told me that they might indeed have a different approach. They modeled several new ways to look at how leaders can experience information. In short, they made me wiser.

Access

I had been devoted to Microsoft Outlook for quite a while, once racking up five thousand e-mail messages a year, not counting newsletters, which would have added thousands more. All of this felt very up-to-date as long as I was sending huge numbers of messages and filing those I received on my hard drive. Unconsciously, I had simply replicated the paper files of an earlier decade. No wonder Microsoft uses tiny, yellowish folder icons to represent how their software stores our files. After several years of feeding it various documents, my computer's Research folder bulged with hundreds of megabytes of truths and trends. My formerly paper-oriented addiction had simply shifted to an electronic form, which kept information in a much smaller container (a laptop) while encouraging me to collect more than ever by mainlining the Internet. Paper had been only the gateway "drug." This measure hardly begins to count the words I produced on my own, an inclination that wore out three laptop keyboards in almost as many years.

Then Glen, a young campus pastor on the West Coast, invited me to join Gmail, a new (at the time) and free e-mail application offered by search engine powerhouse Google. With Glen's help, I began to understand that the Archive function in Gmail, which allowed me to save all my conversations online, represented (for me) a new kind of relationship with information. Because the notion of comprehensive mastery of any field seems more like fiction every day, the information I really need is what it takes to *access* other information. Not having tons of paper or electronic files before my eyes made me feel a little helpless, as if suddenly stripped of the tools of my trade. But the damage was done. The Archive feature, the ability to search the whole Internet with one click, led to the eventual discovery of social bookmarking sites such as Flickr.com that now allow me to use the access principle not just to consume content but to create and publish it to the planet. In the end, Glen's advice about access turned out to be not just information, but wisdom.

Commodity vs. Utility

This transition revealed the fact that my young friends and I have almost totally divergent theories of how information works in the world. To me and much of my generation, information functions like a commodity, a product or service to be sought out, stored, and used to add value to my ministry. Just as coal is discovered with difficulty, mined at great expense, stored carefully, and then distributed only in very controlled ways to appropriate end users like power plants, the data I require to lead seem scarce in supply and laborious to acquire. The value of the refined product, whether a sermon illustration or graphic to be inserted into a slide, is extremely high, given the time and equipment it takes to sort through mountains of nonessentials to find what I ultimately need. Data of such importance deserves to be treasured, claiming the ultimate honor of being stored for possible future use. Unlike my younger friends who feel that information often seeks them out, I seek it out so that I have control.

My reverse mentors have often expressed disbelief that I actually found this model compelling. From their perspective, information functions more as a *utility*. In other words, they experience it like water, which is available in relative abundance across the planet and requires no more effort than standing in the rain to acquire. It is not a coincidence that some clusters of computers are now referred to as "clouds," meaning they are too complex and interactive to be thought of only as networks and may represent the only way to keep up with the exponential growth of information.[4] With data flowing almost literally like water, the Internet natives who tutor me think of accessing it not as mining for coal but simply as turning on a faucet. Although I might take a long-haul view of a certain statistic needed for a training seminar, carefully preserving it like an exhibit at the Smithsonian, they take a *real-time* approach that regards this week's vital statistic as next week's Trivial Pursuit question. As long as access is maintained, storage and mastery are greatly diminished in importance. As fifteen-year-old student Leslie put it, "Why should I memorize dates for history (class)? I can just Google it."[5] The potential risks involved in this point of view are unnerving for older people who tend to be unaware of the risks inherent in their own perspective.

R-mentors such as Joel and Adam, often without even know-ing it, helped sensitize me to those risks and benefits through an appreciation of their way of doing things. For example, my talks became more spontaneous in the sense that the research behind them represented more almost-real-time discoveries, often through an e-mail newsletter or blog read just hours before, or in the form of a spontaneous conversation (in one case at an airport on the way to an event) that offered a new way of looking at the subject of talks on the missional church. One presentation for pastors was developed by asking a group of their peers in another state, "What should I say to pastors?" This group interview took place just seventy-two hours prior, making me more a facilitator of peer mentoring than an expert from out of town with all the answers.

Perspective

I notice that my R-mentors scrupulously avoid using the phrase "information superhighway." They would not refer to the Internet this way any more than I would call a library an "infor-mation warehouse." The "superhighway" expression originally referred to the dramatic way in which the Internet could accel-erate the pace at which people exchanged messages and files. Compare the near-instant arrival of an e-mail with the multiday sojourn of a handwritten letter through the postal system, or the convenience of placing a mobile phone call right now, rather than waiting to find a pay phone in a glass cube. In fact, when I asked a small group of young adults if they had ever written a letter or been in a telephone booth, each had to pause to think about the question and then responded in the affirmative, but in a way that said, "I must have, but it was a long time ago."

The change here is more than just faster hardware. For Internet natives, information has always been fast and technol-ogy always at hand, so their attitude toward handling both tends to differ from that of leaders my age. One research project, for example, tasked Millennials with "scaffolding the learning" of older educators by mentoring them in technological tasks such as creating videos. The teaming of old and young proved to be a positive experience for both groups as well as productive for the grad students in learning their teaching profession, offering the win-win situation commonly reported in studies of reverse mentoring.[6] But achieving these outcomes surfaced a substantial difference in how the young tutors and their older students approached the learning task.

The Millennial students hesitated at first to engage older protégés, but they were utterly comfortable with the hardware and software, having spent their childhood working with them. This level of comfort is understandable when a sixteen-year-old in 2007 was:

- One when Super Nintendo was released and the CD-ROM was invented
- Five when the Internet entered almost every home and PlayStation was released
- Eight when Windows 98 was launched
- Eleven when PlayStation 2, GameCube, and Xbox were released and DSL gained popularity

Seventeen-year-old Zuri typified this kind of attitude by acknowledging that "I chat so much online, right now my time on my buddy list says I have been online for three days! That's how much I love the Internet. The best thing is being able to reach your friends at the click of a mouse."[7] This insight into the Gen Y mind exemplifies the shift from what technology forecaster Paul Saffo has called "coach potato" to "mouse potato."[8]

The merger of these two cultures in the reverse mentoring project revealed that the young mentors favored working with technology by "messing around"; that is, they fearlessly embraced trial and error as the normal path of discovering the potential of hardware or software. The graduate students, however, who preferred step-by-step instructions, were so "terrified" of breaking something that they seldom considered the possibility of discovery on which their R-mentors thrived. The older protégés regarded technology as a part of *work*, while the young treated it more as *play*, consequently possessing a less serious attitude. As Joey, one of the mentors, put it, "The grad students think differently than we do. They don't like to make mistakes. They want it perfect the first time. They should see the cool stuff we've done that started as a mistake." Dora, a practicing teacher, reflected, "We learned that the kids could help us even though they're younger, much younger, than we are."[9]

Initial communication problems were overcome by the growth of mutual respect and cultivation of an intuition on the part of the young mentors for sensing when and how their older mentees needed help. I found this experience replicated by a middle-aged woman who told me how much she enjoyed being in nursing school with younger people, but that when she had asked other students how to make her new iPod work, one of them simply handed it back with the advice "play with it." Like the protégés learning to make videos, she did not know what questions to ask because her point of view on the hardware was out of sync with the culture for which it had been designed.

In encounters like this, my R-mentors have taught me that possessing a device or hoarding multiple gigs of information means little without some kind of perspective on it. For example, it is one thing for me to own an iPod Nano or to read that only 10 percent of teenagers now wear wristwatches. It is another thing to have a sense of *why* these devices and trends exist and what they mean. For instance, young people I interviewed told me that their nearly universal ownership of cell phones (all of which contain clocks) made watches simply unnecessary. But something more profound also finds expression in this small trend. In a twenty-four, seven world, where Taco Bell now offers a "fourth meal" because three are no longer enough, I expect to have my needs met whenever they occur. What's the point in owning a watch when my life happens "whenever"? In effect, then, we're talking about many, perhaps most, young citizens having something like a Personal Time Zone (PTZ) with everything that this implies. For example, how do ministry leaders schedule meetings, whether for a house church or a megachurch? When is the right time when every time is right? Without perspective, the information helps, but not enough.

Wisdom

With the option of asking God for anything, King Solomon chose above all else to plead for the wisdom to lead.[10] That's a prayer Christian leaders should pray every day. However, in addition to *imparted* wisdom like the kind that Solomon received, the Scriptures also refer to the *imported* variety gained through learning, experience, and observation. This sounds fine until we attempt to lead in an information economy that feels like standing at the bottom of Niagara Falls trying to capture a drink of water in a tin cup. Reading ten hours a day at an average pace, for example, it would take over a year to digest the leadership books published in just the last couple of years. Today's expertise, then, rapidly morphs into tomorrow's obsolescence. Wasn't I playing Pong just yesterday? But this very sense that data and hardware clock out at a faster pace all the time drives both the supply of information and the demand for it. One educator depicts college graduates as receiving more facts in a year than their grandparents did in a lifetime; and he projects that, to remain competitive, many workers will need to accumulate the learning equivalent of a master's degree every seven years—the same amount of time it takes for all that is known to double.[11]

Faced with this onslaught, those who feel called to lead can find themselves either sinking into discouragement or exhausting themselves trying to stay current.

There is another option: transitioning out of the information economy into the *wisdom* economy, in which the highest priority is combining access with perspective to produce action. Although I have been doing research in many forms since the Nixon administration, my R-mentors have a culture-current sense of which information I need, what it means, and how to use it. One of them, for instance, pointed me to social bookmarking Websites like del.icio.us (where users post their Internet findings in an interactive public venue), helping me to understand that my "favorites" list was an anachronism and that information now functioned as a medium of social exchange, a form of "currency" that people trade as a way to build relationship networks that can lead to anything from small conversations to large events.

Reflecting on the prevalence of seventeen- and eighteen-year-old researchers in Silicon Valley, freelance youth and culture journalist Elizabeth Weil summarizes the situation: "Forget the experience curve. The most powerful force in business is the inexperience curve. Young companies, born on the right side of the digital divide, are running circles around their older, richer, slower rivals. If you want your company to think outside the box, why not learn by working with people who don't know there is a box?"[12] Inexperience as a source of wisdom? The very thought of it can make leaders my age feel as though their ministry is *so* five minutes ago. But those who are open to incorporating the unique perspective of the young, with their own experience, will find that being wise is much better than just being informed. As Mary, one of the teacher protégés of the Gen Y mentors, put it, "I was impressed with how much of their knowledge they were willing to share. Nothing was protected; they were just there for us." A peer, Elisa, added simply, "We grew to trust them," while one of the student mentors, a "more experienced junior peer," commented in a focus group that "I learned adults were willing to listen to what I had to say." With this kind of friendship in place, everyone is wiser regardless of the skills or information involved.

The Truth Is Out There

How can we know so much and understand so little? Older leaders who accept the paradox of being more informed but less wise as a real risk factor can increase their access and gain new perspective. In combination, these elements can lead to effective action in the world in which the mission of God happens (as opposed to the world we grew up in, or the world as we would like it to be). The first steps in this migration involve premises like this one: *the truth is out there*. Even though I value the insights available in resources like books (or I wouldn't be writing this one), the truth is also found inside people. My cultural background in modernity consistently implied that personal reflections produced only subjective opinions, while reason and observation furnished a superior, objective source of truth. My experience with reverse mentors convinced me to bring a blank tablet to every class I teach to record the things the students will *teach me* through their discussions and comments. I maintain the discipline to this day and have filled many pages with new insights that I would never have identified on my own. Without diminishing the value of formal inquiries, then, I have found much "truth" in the experiences of people I meet, often by accident. A thirtysomething theoretical mathematician sitting beside me on an airliner changed my idea of the future with a three-minute description of research into prime number theory that will support "quantum computing" powerful enough to render encryption of any kind on the Internet impossible. I could not even imagine what *would* become possible. I also cannot imagine the book (*The Idiot's Guide to Prime Number Theory*) that would have made these concepts accessible to a person whose math grades were as woeful as mine. The key to our conversation was her ability to answer my questions in a way that translated enormously abstract concepts into concrete examples that I could grasp. She had to be there personally for that to happen. When God wanted to reveal redemption to us, a person was sent to embody the message. Conversations like this help me understand why.

A second new premise is that *I will never learn anything by talking*. So I seldom miss an opportunity to "interview" most of the people I meet. Their lives (I want to know *who* they are), their calling (I want to know what they *love*), their information stock (I want to know *what* they know), and their personal network (I want to know *whom* they know) are to me like the departments of a large library. Spending many hours buying coffee and listening to leaders young and old across the country has given me the opportunity to be challenged by the things they know ("Are you into social bookmarking sites?" My first thought was, "social what?") and by the wisdom they possess ("When we tried an artsy look with our young adult ministry, we lost the blue-collar kids and the jocks."). As a child of the information economy, I found these friends helping me to start crossing over into the wisdom economy, and with it a new way of looking at things.

Perhaps the crucifying level of self-control that it takes to act on these two principles is itself a form of wisdom. I struggle with both areas every day, but when faced with a need for access or perspective I am now trying to ask myself: *Whom do I know who knows about this?* In a sense, then, wisdom recommends that I think of myself as a broker or networker of information rather than a repository or fountainhead. This attitude is an emerging form of "expertise," as well as a new source of credibility for the old among the young. In a reverse mentoring partnership, then, it *is* about who you know.

When communication professor Jim Towns asked a college class, "If you could call a meeting of the world, what would you like to teach them?" the responses moved him to realize: "I was learning from them. They were mentoring me! The knowledge and wisdom went beyond academics into inspiration and principles for living. They taught and/or reinforced in me astute insights in the areas of principles of living, overcoming difficulties and compassion."[13] This kind of learning comes from being quiet long enough to hear it.

6

RELATIONSHIP

Befriending Beyond Our Peers

Jason would stop by my office unannounced once or twice a month. As a seminary professor, I often worked with students on a one-to-one basis, but his visits were always fascinating because of his wide-ranging interests in literature and pop culture. I recognized some of his references to film and music, but most of them felt unfamiliar and even alien. Very soon I realized that Jason's consumption of media vastly exceeded my own and celebrated an edgy, independent vibe that made my taste for *Law and Order* reruns seem quaint.

By sheer contrast, he helped me understand that as a Boomer I saw television in the central position among the media that made up the "entertainment" category of my life. For Jason, however, film, music, and other media forms seemed less a category and more like the core of his life, expressing both his personality and his priorities. He was a walking iPod, able to give me detailed reviews of artists, albums, and whole musical genres (most of which I had never heard of) at a moment's notice. It was all so natural for him to describe, and so much an act of will power for me to grasp. Jason was a native to his downtown, indie rock, graphic novel subculture, and I was the immigrant. I read books to grasp what Jason knows every morning when he wakes up. This distinction places him in the role of one of my cultural guides, what ethnographers call "informants," an indigenous person willing to teach the language and customs of the group, especially those not recorded in writing.

Jason's role as cultural interpreter took concrete form the day he offered to take me to a local store selling used music CDs. Having spent hours discussing bands such as Death Cab for Cutie and Snow Patrol, I jumped on the chance for a deep dive into the burgeoning indie rock subculture. At the store, we spent an hour walking up and down the bins of plastic CD cases, all filed alphabetically by artist in upright rows, a postmodern Dewey Decimal System. Like a museum docent, Jason moved effortlessly from one band to the next, explaining their background, the origin of their name, how so many of them owed at least a part of their sound to another band called Radiohead, and why their latest album was "too commercial." If he had presented a syllabus for this experience, the first course objective might have read something like this: "Teach professor Earl just enough about music to drop band names (The Killers) during presentations, but not so much that he starts freaking out or feeling obsolete." Amidst our tour, I picked up several albums for purchase and immediate transfusing into my iPod (given to me by a group of young staff pastors from Minnesota as an R-mentoring perk). Even though I still enjoy the music and have added to the collection, I also remember the crucial lesson taught that day by my R-mentor: the most important thing about one's musical preferences is to be informed about them to such a level of detail that one might even be considered a "snob" of sorts.

Another immigrant person might scoff at Jason's lessons, thinking them trivial, disposable, or the province of an insignificant social group that we risk nothing in ignoring. I suspect that a dismissive attitude sometimes serves as the drug of choice for treating misunderstanding complicated by the fear of impending obsolescence. The issue extends far beyond the Anglo middle class. An American missionary acquaintance serving in Africa, for example, telephoned one day to say he had been asked to lead a new young adult congregation in a large city there primarily because older African leaders found these young people so perplexing, so unlike themselves, that they wanted nothing to do with them. Perhaps he represented a neutral third party, or seemed young enough to understand them, but neither interpretation changes the fact that the senior generation outsourced its own children. Our conversation made me wonder if it will be possible to win them back later. Would I look forward to a reunion with an older generation that was willing to welcome me as soon as I had become more like them?

This chapter deals with the process of benefiting from these dissimilarities by using them as the basis for some of our most challenging and interesting friendships. It is difficult to imagine any human relationship that does not have at least some cross-cultural elements, and my relationships with the Jasons of the world feature many. The challenge is to find the grace to exert a transforming effect on one another by drawing on the kind of love and humility that cross-cultural friendships require. No wonder that, after a huge literature review, one scholar of mentoring points to "the importance of being able to 'get along'" as an indispensible ingredient for effectiveness.[1] If relating to the unlikely involves such commonsense thinking and is so critically important, why do such relationships remain so challenging?

PDAs and VCRs

A high-ranking officer speaking on this issue within military organizations compares the generation "born with PDAs in their hands and the generation with VCRs that continue to blink 12:00."[2] In the absence of unlikely friendships, VCR leaders and PDA leaders both end up feeling marginalized, the former because they fear creeping obsolescence and the latter because they feel deprived of the personal connection that gives their work meaning. One not-old leader who mentors the young bemoans the resulting pattern: "The temptation is for older to hang with older and for younger to do the same." A colleague adds that "every day I get a little more disconnected. . . .

Sometimes it feels as though things have changed so rapidly just to keep me off balance or on the edge of the conversation."[3] Many of my peers would add an "Amen" to this lament, and at times they approach me in private asking for an explanation of young adult customs they find intimidating or incomprehensible. With the barbarians at the gates, the likelihood of our benefiting from getting to know each other easily drops almost to the vanishing point, for two simple reasons.

"I Don't Know You"

Unfamiliarity with another's culture besets every new relationship. In fact, working through this barrier to establish more recognizable common ground makes up much of the relationship-building process itself. However, PDA and VCR leaders are separated by more than simple lack of exposure. Dozens of business-oriented books, Websites, and consultants are devoted to the subject of generational issues and the possibility of enhancing performance through what amounts to cooperation in the office. But after years of such training (much of it very useful), the PDA-VCR gulf remains a hindrance to mutual learning. We simply have different interests, issues, and friends. The economy we share works very hard at keeping us together in easy-to-market homogeneous cohorts, in touch with consumption but out of touch with each other. Many Christian ministries inadvertently parallel this fragmentation by seldom bringing all the age groups together in any truly interactive forum.

For example, imagine how my cohort would react to Stanford graduate MC Lars, who describes himself as a "post-punk laptop rap artist," and his song "iGeneration:"

And people tried to put us down

When iTunes bumped a post-Cold War sound

My generation sat at the Mecca of malls,

Times Square, I'm there, Viacom installs

So we hit the net while the Trade Center fell

New York met Hollywood, we ran like hell

No Vietnam for us, yo, Iraq it's on

So who agreed upon this cowboy Genghis Khan?

The choice made, baby. Hey we'd take it back

logged in dropped out, MTV took track

They sold it back to us and claimed no correlation

The iMac, iPod, iGeneration

And I'm waiting for the day we can get out

The world is ours, that's the story no doubt

Want to be more than info super highway traffic

want to be more than a walking demographic!

[CHORUS]

"Hey! You're part of it" Talking about the iGeneration

"Yeah! You're part of it" Talking about my iGeneration

See the iGeneration knew organization

meant optimization and unification

When imagination gave participation

In creation of culture a manifestation

The Berlin Wall fell and out we came

The post-Cold War kids laid claim to AIM.

LOL, OMG, yo, BRB. Space, colon, dash, closed parenthesis

We sat at our laptops and typed away,

and found that we each had something to say

Web-logged our fears, our hopes and dreams

Individuated by digital means

Fiber optic lenses, DVD, Coca Cola, Disney and Mickey D's.

Flat mass culture, the norm that took hold

I hope I die before I get sold

[REPEAT CHORUS]

This is the I-N-T-E. R-N-E-T ge-na-ra-tion, see?

This is the I-N-T-E. R-N-E-T ge-na-ra-tion, see?[4]

The iGeneration, "a group born and raised in the time of the Ninja Turtles, cassette tapes and new wave music, who now live in the age of Desperate Housewives, Sidekicks and screamo bands," understandably unnerves some of the older generations, especially those who lead organizations.

This artist's approach to his music, for example, represents a new set of rules that run counter to the patterns that are convenient for development of large-scale conventional institutions. Performing globally with only a laptop and his songs, Lars builds audience and promotes his own record label using the new rules, "rather than fall into the major label glut. He sees little need for the traditional label trappings and would rather storm his own trail through the Internet even encouraging file-sharing as a means of promoting his music."[5] MC Lars offers a window into something more than niche music or exploiting the marketing potential of pirating one's own songs. His preference to "storm his own trail," particularly when using the Internet as the vehicle, represents an approach to life and work quite alien to leaders my age for whom the precedent is to do what the boss tells us. This generational rep masters technologies beyond our grasp, expresses experiences we never had, and accomplishes it all essentially using one laptop and the Web. The natural temptation when encountering a PDA person like this, echoed in many interviews with leaders of my generation, pulls them toward minimizing the example ("it's just technology"), or the personhood ("they'll grow out of it"), or the contribution ("their following is tiny").

"I Fear You"

Feeling the power of the temptation to marginalize those I don't understand, I sense that something deeper operates within it: *generation shock*, the anxiety produced when a tribe so unlike my own seems to threaten much of what I spent my life building, not by frontal assault but by the sheer brute force of its irrelevance to them. In other words, many Boomers fear that we are about to be ignored to death. Perhaps, then, more than a lack of information blocks the path to friendship between those who think of John Kennedy's death as an assassination and those who think of it as a small plane crash. One survey asked American workers if they agreed with the prediction that "Baby Boomers will have to surrender power before they are ready" in the face of technical mastery displayed by the young. *The Economist* reports that "two-thirds of the respondents agreed but, tellingly, nearly as many thought that the trend was worrying."[6] Some of this anxiety is well founded, as depicted in the film *In Good Company* when the middle-aged advertising executive played by Dennis Quaid finds himself, at the peak of his career, reporting to a new boss half his age, played by Topher Grace. This fictional account is not far from the reality that some older leaders face and that many of them fear.

How does the iGeneration, then, find a seat at the leadership table—and would they want one? Many of them find the way we do business tragically out of sync with the world to which they are native, and we often return the favor by framing them as so out of sync with how things run in the "real world" that the thought of their taking over (or, worse, muscling us out in the process) makes mutual respect harder to come by than it should be. Consequently, any learning between the two cohorts often devolves into not much more than giving or following orders at worst or an exchange of information at best. This cycle demonstrated itself recently in a classroom discussion between an older missionary and his younger peer, with the former demanding respect for his age group on the basis of their position and experience, and the latter asserting that ignoring the senior person's method in favor of new approaches constitutes innovation, *not* disrespect. In this scenario the argument begins, but the learning ends.

Unlikely Friends

When Bruce, then a twentysomething youth pastor, offered in the mid-1990s to introduce me to e-mail by recommending Juno software for my 486sx desktop computer, I wondered: Wasn't I the boss? Shouldn't I be teaching him? The same prospect appears when Natalie (age five) explains the operation of her digital camera to me, or when her brother Joshua (age ten) tutors me in video game tactics. The challenge stems not just from what they know, because I already take digital photos, but from *when* they knew it—fifty years younger than I did. Their comfort level with technology and interactive media (and what they represent) approaches my comfort level with refrigerators and automobiles.

Dropping my defenses so that these very young friends can teach me requires more than asking for information or instruction, as if I were scheduling a piano lesson or going to hear a lecture. When I sent my first e-mail (which went across the hall to Bruce's office using a dial-up connection), I still believed that my software actually routed the message through Juno—Alaska. I marveled at a technology powerful enough to send what still seemed like just an electric letter almost to the Arctic before rushing it back to Bruce's inbox in Florida. This experience joined a string of others to build a friendship, one that involved the uncomfortable realization that the city of Juno did not serve as the international e-mail "switchboard," a quaint analogy I had borrowed from telephony to make sense of the Internet. E-mail led to the World Wide Web, which led to meeting the iGeneration.

No wonder MIT's Edgar Schein contends that, despite years of change management training, most organizations still manage to avoid real transformation. He attributes this failing to the fact that the ability to challenge the basic assumptions on which we operate escapes the vast majority of leaders, with the results looking more like tweaking than transformation. The kind of learning that really changes things is a "coercive process," painful, challenging, and fraught with anxiety.[7] Many older leaders relate to this description in very personal terms and overlook the force that overcomes learning anxiety: a vision of the potential for our ministries available through friendship with the unlikely. Friendships come in a variety of formats and depths, but all of them help Christian leaders experience the power of collaboration and the wisdom of a new perspective. One fifty-eight-year-old minister learning from an R-mentor over the Internet put it this way: "RM makes an old guy feel useful in today's kingdom. It challenges me and sharpens me."

Sometimes, these friendships can even be borrowed. When preparing to travel to the West Coast on a field research trip to document some innovative ministries, for example, I realized that simply landing in California meant very little without some personal referrals for leaders to interview and venues to record. The president of my seminary simply opened what in those days we called a Rolodex and I discovered that, even in his very senior role, he maintained a large network of younger friends, largely composed of former students from a university in California. Responding to a presidential request, one of those students, David Trotter, who was living in the area wrote: "I would be glad to spend some time with you and more importantly get you connected to leaders in the area. . . . If you are having a hard time getting in to any of these guys, let me know and I can try to 'bust through the barrier.' How does that sound? What else can I do for you?" Supplying a list of around ten leaders to interview (including Spencer Burke and Dan Kimball), he concluded, "If your schedule gets full, don't worry about having to hold off on hanging with me . . . I just want to be of whatever help I can." VCR leaders need to understand this willingness of the young to help and the tangible benefits of developing such alliances. David's referrals, made possible by a leader who valued the young enough to consider them "network-worthy," changed the course of my life and ministry by putting me in touch with iGeneration leaders. With similar graciousness, they explained their vision of the church's future and taught me the value of looking for that future by walking with the church rather than just reading about it. They bear much of the responsibility for our new adventure in church planting in Berkeley, California. Perhaps they culti-vated so much interest in the future in our hearts that we simply needed to go become a part of it.

Unlikely collaborations of this kind in the for-profit sector also serve as case studies depicting the possibilities for ministry leaders. International computer equipment and banking firms, for exam-ple, have found that treating customers as "co-inventors" rather than merely buyers of products changes the dynamic of their busi-ness. Accustomed to relying on demonstrations and simulations to pitch their goods and services, these firms lacked a precedent for sharing with their customers the internal tools actually used to develop those products. But adopting this unorthodox practice proved immediately rewarding. After freely giving customers the mathematical tools used to design their firm's complex financial instruments, one investment executive admits, "Frankly, [our clients] didn't fully trust either us or our simulations. It wasn't until we started giving them the simulation tools we used our-selves that they took us seriously."[8] Similar reports across a variety of industries confirm the value of collaboration of this sort that defies conventional expectations. One major automobile manufacturer, for example, designed a popular new model in response to customer insight at a Website designed for this purpose. The same company stretched even further by hiring a lead designer for one of its lines who had never worked on automobiles before to bring fresh thinking to the enterprise.

In both cases, the value in the relationship results from the *dissimilarity* of those involved, rather than from how they mirror each other. Once again, the church appears to offer few examples of leading the way on this issue, but this state of affairs need not be permanent. After a talk on this subject for a small group of Southern Baptist leaders, an employee of a large computer company approached me with the admonition to write a book that would help Christians lead the way on R-mentoring in the marketplace. He saw the need not just in the ranks of vocational ministry but even more so among those they serve. This very sincere man seemed to say that he simply had so few Christian examples from which to draw inspiration that he felt doomed to wait until his company developed an R-mentoring program and then, perhaps in ten or fifteen years, someone in ministry leadership might also try it out. We simply cannot wait that long.

And we do not need to. Most studies of reverse mentoring (although few in number) find the relationship to impart substantial mutual benefits out of the very dissimilarity that can make it so daunting to begin. In fact, one Swedish telecom firm insists that to qualify as an R-mentor its gifted young employees must meet the main qualification of being "outspoken."[9] Similarly, a Belgian engineering firm searches for R-mentors who *fail* to match the profile of their average employee, specifically meaning that they must meet two out of these three criteria: "non-Belgian, non-male and non-engineer."[10] Again, the advantage of the R-mentoring relationship comes from a sometimes intimidating disparity, not from soothing uniformity.

An outspoken R-mentor who is non-me will by the nature of our diverse backgrounds offer the benefit of a new point of view I might never have conceived of without this person. The new viewpoint can spark understanding and creativity by pushing me beyond the perimeter of my own ideas.

These case studies pose the question of whether we, like the American auto designers and the Belgian engineers, possess the humility and the faith to embrace those who take a new path to the same destination. I believe we can find the grace to reach out, not because a mentoring system demands it, but because simple friendship allows it. One older minister summarizes his own journey in these terms:

> I am becoming more aware of how badly I need to have younger people around me to keep me somewhat current on trends and mores. It is not uncommon for me to show up a day late on some trend. . . . Actually that's OK, because I do not need to be in every stream of conversation. I know it is not personal; it is just the pace and the herd moving on to new and different grazing fields. I suggest that a revolution is needed; old guys working with young guys in wisdom areas and young guys working with old guys helping them to be contemporary and wise about things of the moment.

As some leaders criticize the young and others wait for elaborate mentoring systems, we dare not let the opportunity to extend ourselves in friendship slip away. This simple spiritual act affords the vehicle to bond with the young, giving them the opportunity to shock us, provoke us, and delight us.

Sometimes I am asked questions about the possible risk factors in reverse mentoring. Generally, these inquiries sound like this: "What if my confidence is betrayed?" "What if my young teacher treats me in a patronizing or condescending way?" "What if I just don't get anything out of it?" These questions sound like challenges to the whole RM idea, but they actually illustrate the value of its core feature: friendship. Issues within the relationship can be dealt with in exactly the same way that friends would settle any concern. For example, many of my interviews with younger leaders have involved the issue of how widely their views would be disseminated beyond just me, given the sometimes controversial nature of the subjects we discussed. As I learned from them and increasingly wanted to share what I was hearing with others, I had to keep in mind that friends don't expose each other to unnecessary risks, so I often kept their names out of my presentations and writings. This practice did not come at their request but simply evolved out of the quality of the relationship. Effective reverse mentoring, then, is the result of a meaningful friendship. If we know how to have real friends, we can manage RM using all the same skills of conversation, honesty, and integrity. Perhaps reverse mentoring is attempted so seldom in ministry leadership because we are better at building organizations than building relationships.

Lost

Working together for several years, an almost-fifty Carlton Cuse and the midthirties Damon Lindelhoff produce and write *Lost*, one of the most popular television programs of the last decade. The Harvard-educated Cuse offered Lindelhoff his first writing job in television, creating a close partnership of mentor and protégé. However, both men contribute to creation of the program out of their "complementary talents," Cuse says. "We see the show very similarly. There's very little we don't fundamentally agree on, whether it's the direction of the show, the aesthetics or the stories we want to tell people."[11] Similarly, Christian leaders can grow through unlikely relationships because those involved practice mutual respect and basic agreement on the story line.

The lessons Jason taught me during his guided tour of the used CD store found their power in this way. The outlet's clientele that afternoon consisted mainly of men in their early twenties dressed a lot like the musicians featured on the album covers they browsed. My awkward feelings of being out of place actually served as a learning platform, putting me in touch with a simple piece of intercultural wisdom: when I feel out of place, the less I say the better. My social angst also suggested the annoying corollary that the same vow of silence may apply when I *do* feel in place.

Jason's services as a tour guide afforded me a fledgling sensitivity to indie rock music and metrosexual fashion, both (for now) global artifacts of the post-Boomer generation. Our cultural immersion also furnished a venue for the practice of something more important: unlikely friendship. He and I grew up in different places (Mexico, Pennsylvania), in different generations (Gen X, Boomer), with different tastes (graphic novels, Tom Clancy), and met at the seminary in different roles (student, professor).

My almost-accidental relationship with Jason broke with the customs of my tribe and offered a glimpse of the power of simple friendship. After five years of taking corporate executives out of their offices and into cultural immersion experiences, Andy Ford observes that "the simplest, easiest, shortest solution is sometimes farthest away from the people who know the most."[12] My own experience certainly lends credibility to this conclusion, suggesting that VCR leaders consider turning to PDAs to receive the kind of education that changes things, and to broaden the opportunities to mentor them in return.

Part Three

EXPERIENCING PRACTICALITY

7

EVANGELISM

Learning from Outsiders

Standing on the asphalt of the parking lot, I met Jim, a young man assigned by the car rental company to help me fill out the necessary paperwork and talk me into upgrading. As he and I went through the practiced motions of selecting fueling options and declining overpriced insurances, Jim asked the reason for my visit to California. I told him that I was in town to speak at a missions convention for a local church. He remarked that his rental agency did a lot of bookings for missionary trips of various kinds, so I followed up by asking how he had arrived in California; his accent betrayed roots in another part of the country.

He spoke of growing up in an evangelical Christian home on the Atlantic Coast, of traveling west to attend college, and then crashing into ideas that shook his faith so badly that the residue consisted of just "a lot of questions." The pained expression on his face told me that Jim's once-simple beliefs now felt like a pile of rubble, reduced to fragments by a world he never counted on. Just minutes into what started as a business-only relationship, Jim and I talked of spirituality as if these conversations happened all the time. He seemed to respond positively to the lack of any attempt to conceal my ministry vocation, typically the last thing I wanted to volunteer because of the possibility that our talk would go no further than his stereotypes. Perhaps because I answered his question directly about the reason for my trip, stereotypes never seemed to hinder our talk.

Jim's first spiritual question to me was not, "Where should I go to church?" but "Do you know a Website that will help me answer my questions?" Approaching him with a recommendation for any other form of ministry would almost certainly mean a dead end. Not everyone is ready for a church visit, a small group, or a one-to-one counseling session. The Web seemed to Jim a safe first step for reexploring the possibilities of faith without trying to force him to abandon the doubts that kept him in self-imposed exile from any Christian community. I was embarrassed by my inability to give him more than a URL or two on the spot, not being prepared yet to think of the Web as the evangelistic tract of the twenty-first century. Offering what I did have available, I gave Jim the name of the church where I was speaking and also passed along a business card, inviting him to e-mail me with questions or comments. I never heard from him, but my encounter with Jim made me more aware of people all around us waiting to have similar conversations—if they get to ask the first question and then do most of the talking.

This chapter concerns the value of listening to outsiders, both in living an evangelistic life and strategizing evangelism for organizations. The apostle Paul advised the church at Colossae to "be wise in the way you act toward outsiders; make the most of every opportunity. Let your conversation be always full of grace, seasoned with salt, so that you may know how to answer everyone."[1] Reaching "outsiders" effectively, then, requires more than just initiative on the personal level and strategic decisions on the organizational level, both of which are vital in their own way. The very people who we hope will consider the good news about Jesus can themselves offer a form of reverse mentoring, not to change the nature of that good news but to help the church understand how they hear it. This rapport encourages conversations "full of grace, seasoned with salt," in which the gospel seems credible and the outsider's heart can open.

This kind of process in the corporate world carries the label of *backward or weak socialization*, using newcomers, in the words of Stanford engineering professor Robert Sutton, not as trainees but as "'consultants' from the outside, much like those hired as professionals, but much cheaper."[2] Even though our goal is not to cut costs, the logic for ministry leaders is similar: outsiders see things in our lives and ministries that insiders do not, and knowing those things can change how we live and speak our witness in the world. Outsiders also deserve the kind of respect found only when someone listens, and insiders need to learn how to have salty conversations. In the ancient world, salt was a highly valued and versatile commodity, used as a form of currency, a preservative, and a flavor enhancer. In the modern (or postmodern world), the good news gains currency with outsiders when it is flavored with acceptance, understanding, and respect. Good evangelism, then, tastes like grace and prepares outsiders not to answer our questions but to expect us to answer theirs.

Outsiders and Insiders

The willingness to listen does not come easily. Countless schools offer courses and degree programs in communication, compared to only a relative handful of classes on "listening." Given the choice, most of us (including me) prefer the sending side to the receiving in any interaction. This monologue penchant sometimes finds expression among Christians sharing their faith individually or corporately. These commendable efforts usually bear fruit in direct proportion to how responsive they are to the Holy Spirit's leading and how attuned they are to the perspective of the outsider. We learn to follow these leadings by listening to God; we learn to attune ourselves to outsiders by listening to them.

Jesus spent three decades among the people of his nation before beginning three years of public ministry, a ten-to-one ratio. He listened to the Father and spoke the message to the people among whom he spent his life. No wonder the crowds listened to him, as the gospel of Mark says, "with delight."[3] Today, three years of training is supposed to prepare us for thirty years of service, also a ten-to-one ratio, but perhaps in the wrong direction. Helping outsiders consider what I once heard George Hunter say were "the Christian possibilities for their lives" requires that we never stop learning. This means we listen to them, first out of love and then out of necessity.

The first lesson in the school of listening is that outsiders hardly constitute a homogeneous people group. Janet and I found this diversity at the sidewalk level during a site visit to a church plant sponsored by two mainline denominations in an eastern city. The congregation met in a large multistory building sitting in the midst of a recently renovated neighborhood that was now a haven for upscale young professionals, an industrial wasteland converted into yuppie heaven. The name of steel companies once common in the region had been replaced by brands such as American Eagle Outfitters and Kenneth Cole.

Visiting a Sunday morning worship service, we discovered a fairly young crowd of around two hundred seated in the round, their chairs on a parquet tile floor, with a communion table in the middle and worship band (including local punk musicians) off to the side. But the most enlightening part of our visit to this two-year-old fellowship happened out on the street. We walked around the neighborhood for about an hour before entering the building just to get a grip on the context and to encounter some of the local citizens in hopes of asking them about the church. In our brief tour, we encountered three kinds of outsiders.

Binocular People

While parking our car, we met Donna and Carl, an African American couple living in an apartment that almost overlooked the church. Asked if they knew about the congregation, they told us of visiting once and enjoying it, especially the brief, humorous plays that served as the signature feature of the worship services. Although neither Donna nor Carl paid a return visit on a Sunday morning, they continued to monitor the church from their nearby vantage point, joking that their observations were like those of someone using "binoculars." This kind of outsider fails to fit the stereotype of the hostile, atheistic ideologue bent on the destruction of all things Christian. With one Gallup survey reporting, for example, that American teens "overwhelmingly seek spiritual growth in their daily lives," the binocular person, friendly toward Christian spirituality but observing from a distance, may represent the spiritual mainstream of our next generation of adults. Reaching these persons will require more than inviting them again to events they have already seen.[4]

Bookstore People

After interviewing Donna and Carl, I stopped into a well-known chain bookstore on the next block. Noticing the almost total lack of customers on a Sunday morning, I greeted the young woman working behind a counter and asked if she knew anything about the church we planned to visit. She looked a little puzzled and then replied curtly that she had never heard of it. Clearly, our conversation was at an end, so I thanked her and walked back out onto the sidewalk. Bookstore people live or work in proximity to a Christian witness just like Binocular people, but they remain oblivious to its presence even when only fifty yards away. Consequently, they do little observing, so their lives proceed as if the Christian community never existed because to them it does not. A friend described this kind of outsider as "so post-Christian they aren't even mad about it anymore." Communicating with Bookstore people means living a life that insinuates a reality bigger than theirs just outside the bookstore, with words and deeds "seasoned with salt."

Bistro People

We also stopped by a franchise coffeehouse across the street and down the block from the church entrance. During the process of ordering our drinks, we started a conversation with the staff comparing favorite films and discovered a mutual preference for the "mockumentary" genre. When I asked the young man and woman behind the counter if they knew of the nearby church, they immediately lit up. The pastors frequented their establishment, stopping in for hours to do research or hold meetings. We got the impression that the coffeehouse was the office-of-choice for the church staff, making it an outpost in the community. One of the employees had visited the church, but only once as research for a school assignment. For Bistro people, geographic proximity shrinks in importance because the Christian community goes to them, creating *relational proximity* that neither the Binocular nor Bookstore people enjoy. As with Jim at the car rental place, who wanted to start his spiritual journey on the Internet, my coffeehouse acquaintances leaned toward starting small, talking with the people who visited them rather than becoming visitors in a larger group.

These three simple examples are not meant to offer a comprehensive description of outsiders. But they do demonstrate the spiritual diversity found in just one hour of doing three brief interviews on two city blocks. Multiply this variety by the other forms of diversity all around us and the potential number of dispositions toward the Christian faith among outsiders very soon exceeds our ability to calculate. Pop singer Sheryl Crow expresses the multiplicity of options she feels just in her own life: "I believe in God . . . I believe in Jesus and Buddha and Mohammed and all those that were enlightened. I wouldn't say necessarily that I'm a strict Christian. I'm not sure I believe in heaven."[5] Engaging a pluralistic culture like this with formulaic monologues that package the gospel as if it were only a set of ideas seems unlikely to gain traction, mainly because this approach assumes that the outsider cares about *my* presentation rather than *our* conversation.

Younger church planters in Japan are experimenting with an alternative method called "listening shops," *kikiya* in their language.[6] Takeshi Takazawa, country resource coordinator for Japan with the Asian Access church planting ministry, explains

the process: "You sit in the middle of the city with a sign. . . .
A lot of people stop and want to talk to you . . . not a lot of
explanation . . . people feel it or experience it. . . . You just listen to the people. . . . As you listen their heart is opened up and
usually they ask you why are you doing this, or what happened
to you. . . . Then that's the opening of sharing your life . . . not
some idea or philosophy or logic. . . . your story merges with
the other person's story. . . . That's how authentic relationship
starts . . . and God works miraculously in that relationship."

The point of this example is to make a case not for a certain method but for the practical value of the instruction found
in James 1:19 that "everyone should be quick to listen, slow to
speak and slow to become angry." This principle offers benefits
beyond prevention of conflict, including a key resource for
expressing God's love to outsiders in faithful, authentic, and
engaging ways. A genuine caring for the outsider is the heart
of this kind of witness, establishing its authenticity by making
the point of the conversation the other person, rather than the
results. In the same way that Jesus died for us when we cared
nothing for him, the listening friend invests in the outsider per
se, regardless of whether the outsider responds to the good news
in our presence. Ironically, then, the fewer our words, the saltier
they may become.

Gina and Bob

Visiting the Sunday morning service of a large Pentecostal
church in northern Europe with a group of friends, we heard
very familiar worship melodies that meant almost nothing
because the lyrics projected on the screen above our heads
were in the language of the country. Attempting to pronounce
these words phonetically in tempo with the music felt awkward
because all of our energy had to be devoted to the exercise, leaving nothing for actually worshipping. We found ourselves on the
inside of the event but the outside of the experience.

Used to international guests, our very gracious hosts supplied headsets powered by infrared beams through which translators would broadcast an English version of the announcements and the sermon. The devices, however, were both insufficient in number and unreliable in operation, resulting in our receiving about three words out of every five. The only remedy we could devise involved passing the few functional headsets back and forth among ourselves every few minutes in hopes of creating some kind of composite of the sermon. Many times after that service I wondered if outsiders experience our events and our witness in the same way: the basic language seems alien and the fragments that come through do not make sense unless someone helps put them together. Back in the United States, when I asked fifteen-year-old Heather, for example, why her peers felt reluctant to attend worship services she responded that the basic barrier had less to do with skepticism than with simple social awkwardness. "When we pray," she explained, "they don't know what to do with their hands."

However, sometimes the grace that seasons our words shows up more quickly than we expect. While at the front of a church multipurpose auditorium one Sunday morning before a service, Janet and I were delighted to see a young woman we knew standing at the back of the room with a cup of coffee in her hand. We went to meet her and brought her to the first row to sit next to Janet during the event. Gina's church background approached a functional zero, so our delight was mixed with surprise. We never expected the exchange of a few e-mails and our recent meeting in another state after years of not seeing each other to result in her driving an hour to attend with us that day. But Janet and I both sensed that our conversations with her some months before served as a sort of reconnection that linked our lives together again.

The service opened with the kind of soft electric rock worship songs common in suburban Anglo churches and proceeded to announcements presented in a video clip, and then to introduction of the speaker. Equipped with a Garth Brooks–style boom mike, I took my place behind the plexiglass pulpit and presented a talk on the grace of God. Although the congregation remained silent throughout the sermon, I noticed that Gina seemed unaware that we generally do not talk to each other during these proceedings, *especially* the sermon (because this proves particularly annoying to those trying to send text messages). Throughout the service, Gina leaned over to speak to Janet, and Janet responded to her each time.

(In our car after the event, I asked my wife why so much conversation took place, and she informed me that their dialogue resulted from Gina's questions about the worship service. She wanted to know things like why the multipurpose building didn't look more like a church, where the worship band played the rest of the week, why the song lyrics appeared on a projection screen, why the auditorium had chairs rather than pews, and so on. Gina liked the coffee in the lobby and the music, found the technology odd, and was disappointed that the church offered nothing for breakfast. In her subculture, inviting someone to an early morning event implied the presence of food as a way of expressing gratitude as well as persuading them to come.)

At the conclusion of my sermon, I walked down a few steps from the platform to the main floor just as Gina came to offer her review. "I liked your talk," she said, "you sounded so normal." Possibly she expected the kind of vehement delivery style that implies in the minds of some audiences the need for "anger management therapy."[7] Gina then concluded her review: "And you gave me a lot to think about." Gina's positive reaction to that Sunday morning, just one step in an ongoing dialogue, resulted from something other than the free coffee, or the rock-and-roll style, or the talk. She responded to Janet's unconditional willingness to listen to and answer her questions in real time. Just as some congregations use sign language experts to interpret their services for the hearing-impaired, Janet used the language of outsiders to interpret that service for the religiously inexperienced. Our Sunday experience was well executed, sincere, and meaningful, but Gina still didn't understand. She needed an interpreter, someone to help her make sense of things. In fact, the need for interpreters increasingly challenges the assumptions behind using these worship forms as a primary means of evangelism. The church we visited had already switched to casual dress for the staff and eliminated "churchy" wording from their presentations. But Gina still didn't get it. She needed a person, a listening person to connect her to the experience.

Our encounter sparked the question of whether Christian organizations should consider offering "interpreters" for outsiders who may look like insiders but certainly do not speak the language. The simple act of listening to their questions might reveal more about how to reach them than many surveys can, and it might do more to bond them to the faith community than many sermons do. Todd Hunter, the head of Alpha USA, a leading evangelism organization, summarizes this dynamic: "If recent research on the attitudes of non-Christians toward Christianity is correct, then the most important skills Christians need to acquire are listening, hearing, and connecting. Connecting with today's seekers requires a new kind of relational honesty."[8] Hearing the outsider, paying attention to questions, and responding with words full of grace will make both living and speaking the gospel credible. Gina will respond to nothing else.

The power of allowing outsiders to mentor us also applies to organizations. Bob, a church planter, for instance, started his new congregation about five years ago with a core group of fifteen. Seven of those people were outsiders to the faith. Most of them were friends of friends asked to help the fledgling leadership team better relate to people not depending on faith in Christ. Meeting in a home, the group launched their life together by studying the gospel of John, with all of them becoming Christians along the way.

However, the combining of insiders and outsiders in the early days of Bob's start-up represented more than an evangelism strategy. Those who found faith during these exploratory meetings developed into the "bringers and gatherers" who involved people from the surrounding neighborhoods in the new faith community. Their presence also helped to shape the DNA of the organization, sensitizing the leadership to the presence of relatively few married people in their neighborhood, meaning that an emphasis on "family ministry" would essentially lock them out. Moreover, the presence of what came to be called a "smoke break" in the middle of worship services (which were known as "gatherings"), allowing time for a pastry and a cup of good coffee, told outsiders that the Sabbath was made for human rhythms and needs. Participation in local art shows sent the message that the church wanted even its facility to be part of the community, not a fortress isolated from it. These traits eventually found their way into the ministry's "Style Guide," something of an church genome project capturing practices as detailed as preferred fonts and premises as sweeping as the strong sense of geographic calling to particular parts of the city.

"Christ following is super messy," Bob comments, going on to contend that the neater protocols of conventional church clean people up only on the outside in most cases. Consequently, with churched imports "[we] put them through the wringer, deprogramming until they realize this isn't about you." These bold moves hardly give Bob an inflated sense of leadership; rather, they have softened him. Describing himself as feeling "unleaderly" at times, Bob jokingly compares himself to Johnny Depp in *Pirates of the Caribbean*, "with that stupid compass that never works." Nonetheless his ministry reaches a very high proportion of outsiders and is exploring another site elsewhere in the city. Regardless of the location, however, "people come with their guts hanging out. . . . The only balm is Jesus; that's old school stuff. You have to pastor in this day and age with *your* guts hanging out. The real ironic thing is how much it changes me." The DNA of that original core group permeates every aspect of Bob's ministry because he possessed the courage to involve them in the kind of tangible ways that allow authentic listening to happen.

Hearing voices from the outside is not always easy. Second Samuel relates, for example, that a man from the clan of the former king of Israel, Saul, confronted King David on the road to Bahurim one day.[9] Shimei cursed the new ruler, pelting him and his entourage with stones and accusations of responsibility for Saul's tragic death, calling the king a "man of blood." The fact that David was on the run from his own son on this day must have made the words hit as hard as the rocks. Resisting the suggestion of Abishai, one of his staff, to behead Shimei for the grave offense of insulting the king, David gave a strange order: "Leave him alone; let him curse, for the Lord has told him to." Although within his rights to execute his tormentor, the king preferred the possibility that the dust and rocks showering down on him carried with them something of God's perspective on his current predicament. David even held out the hope that "the Lord will see my distress and repay me with good for the cursing I am receiving today." Although Shimei represents a social and political outsider, the parallel remains that even the harshest comments about things Christians value can contain insights into how to express them more faithfully and effectively. A man who lives in the neighborhood that Bob's church serves, for example, refuses to attend but maintains an ongoing relationship with Bob and supports the church in covert ways (I suspect so the neighborhood doesn't take notice). Bob's patience in continuing to develop a relationship with a critical person builds the credibility of the ministry every day and encourages his friend to draw closer.

Buy a Dog

Our current challenge of starting a new congregation in Berkeley involves many questions of strategy and resources but will rise and fall on whether I live what I coach. Can I connect with people there in authentic relationships so that listening to them informs the ethos of the whole ministry? Upon hearing we are headed for Berkeley, well-meaning friends sometimes shake their heads out of concern for our calling to such a high-challenge environment, so far from the presumed safety of the Bible Belt. One leader even remarked that "Berkeley has turned its back on God, and God has turned His back on it." Apparently when I said the name of the city, this colleague heard "Nineveh." In fact, a very hip marketing professional confessed to me that, even though he was succeeding everywhere from Dallas to Paris, "I have never been sniffed out like I've been sniffed out in Berkeley . . . [they have] a natural distrust of anyone who appears to be interested in what they're doing." He surmised that the people he met simply intuited that he was "corporate" and wanted nothing to do with the forces he represented. It seems apparent, then, that the act of listening itself, without love, is just another strategy, as attractive to outsiders as the "resounding gong" or "clanging cymbal" of our loveless words.[10]

This challenge came into focus during my final days at the seminary in a telephone conversation with a friend and colleague from the West Coast. I was surprised to discover that she actually lived in the community and knew it well. Although very realistic about the challenges involved, she also described with real affection the many positive features of the town, including its world-class campus and a cultural scene absolutely throbbing with energy. These comments validated the assessment of our friend, Curt Harlow, an experienced West Coast leader who recruited us for the project: "There is no synonym for Berkeley." Wondering how to communicate without parallels or analogies to draw from, I asked my friend for her advice. She made one suggestion: "Buy a dog."

I laughed. She went on to explain that many of Berkeley's citizens feel so fulfilled (almost 85 percent describe the city as an "excellent" or "good" place to live) that spontaneous conversations during simple rituals like a walk in the neighborhood seldom happen. There is simply no felt need, unless that walk involves a dog. Like a babe in arms at the grocery store, an interesting pet opens the way to dialogue about the details of age, name, breed, and so on. A casual chat then can proceed into regular dog conversations, which in turn might develop into a real friendship. This kind of companionship offers the natural network through which Christian witness flows as well as the ideal way to learn the appropriate shape of that witness from outsiders themselves. As in other communities, for instance, the citizenry may hunger more for a sense that their lives *mean* something than feel the need to be saved *from* something.[11] In Christian faith, these two issues both find their resolve at the cross, but expressing this reality in post-Christian settings remains only an abstraction, unless I am willing to listen—and buy a dog.

8

COMMUNICATION

Learning from Listeners

I thought Nick was my friend. Opening one door after another for me both in field ministry and in university settings, he connected me to multiple networks of young leaders and grew into one of my most influential reverse mentors. Through relationship with one of these networks, Nick and I found ourselves sitting on two stools in front of a group of leaders in their twenties and thirties about to start the Q&A scheduled to follow a talk I had just completed. My background in collegiate debating involved enough cross-examination to give me a positive attitude toward questions. I liked them because they gave me more opportunities to talk. Allowing my audiences to remain unaware of this preference formed the foundation of my strategy.

The first question Nick read from the stack of three-by-five cards collected from the audience dealt with how staff pastors and senior pastors get along, an issue that crops up regularly when talking with the former but almost never when talking with the latter. I plunged into my too-long answer, agreeing with the seriousness of the concern, trying to make a few jokes to ventilate the tension, and then wrapping up with some thoughts about possible pathways to reconciliation. Having come to terms with this question several times before in public, I felt pretty good about this answer.

That is, until Nick disagreed with me. "Come on, Earl," he retorted, and proceeded to point out a variety of reasons my response represented more evasion than enlightenment, leaving these young pastors with a false hope for warm friendship with their Boomer leaders. On the outside, I kept smiling and agreed with Nick, who is a national resource on this issue, adding that resolving the problem certainly involved more complications than my answer indicated, and that we all needed to explore other possibilities. Gulp. What's going on here, I wondered? Isn't Nick just supposed to be the MC for this part of the meeting? Then he read the second question from a card and patiently waited until my rhetorical flight came in for a landing. Then he pounced, pointing out gaps in my reasoning and the alternative ways of looking at the subject of the question. I gave a now-forgotten conciliatory reply and realized that Nick saw himself not as a game show host reading questions but as a dialogue partner, one tasked with detecting the presence of anything irrelevant or inauthentic—what the young audience at the time referred to as "cheese" (extreme forms earned the label "Velveeta").

After eight or ten questions I got used to Nick's probing commentary and found myself talking almost as much with *him* as with the group in front of us—and enjoying both. At the end of the evening, I thanked Nick for what felt like the best Q&A session of my life. Nick really was my friend after all. Serving as my interrogator rather than as just a delivery service for the audience's questions, he did the unthinkable: he talked back. The benefit of having my answers contested more than compensated for the higher level of tension in the Q&A that night. In fact, the tension gave the Nick-Earl exchanges an energy that seldom appeared during many other open forum events, which lately were proving to be pretty lifeless. Previously, I thought of the questions themselves as the only fuel for these interactions, but Nick proved that *questioning the answerer* generated both more heat and more light.

The power of the experience derived from the possibility of conflict, but also from the fact that Nick, as he pointed out to me later, only spoke out loud what the audience members were thinking in silence. He served as the ombudsman, the person assigned to speak for people who had no voice in the situation. In his terse responses, I heard thoughts that the format prevented members of the audience from saying to my face. Nick let me know later that my credibility with the group rose because I refused to hide behind my title, position, or even my first answer, displaying openness to being told I was wrong and to engaging that possibility in public.

Through Nick's mediation, then, the audience actually taught me how to express myself in a way they embraced as authentic. This chapter describes both the need and some of the ways in which audiences can serve as reverse mentors for Christian communicators of all kinds, especially those involved in large group settings. One form of credibility operates when others listen to us because we are learners (the knowledgeable), but another form altogether occurs when we learn from listeners, showing them the respect we would like to command for ourselves. To reap respect, sow it.

Listening to Learners

Most training received by Christian communicators owes so much to the field of classical rhetoric that it sometimes seems like little more than a baptized version of a public speaking course. Consequently, the emphasis is on the speaking side of the relationship. In my own churches, a convenient pattern thus emerged: listeners (they) were supposed to pay attention to learners (me) because I possessed knowledge and spiritual insight greater than theirs. My knowledge also carried a special weight in the minds of some because of the authority invested in my position as pastor. This favorable "balance of trade" in our Sunday morning interactions formed the foundation for the preaching relationship. Although I love and believe in preaching and teaching, many contemporary audiences are less likely to trust in authority figures and are more skeptical of anyone's "knowledge," requiring something more than a social exchange based on my superiority. Internet business expert David Siegel, after consulting on hundreds of corporate Websites from start-ups to industry giants, describes a parallel in that arena: "The reality is that most companies have an allegiance not to custom-ers but to existing products and services. . . . If you don't start with the right questions, then you'll end up with the wrong answers."[1] The crucial communication aptitude of the twenty-first century, then, may just be the grace to ask listeners the right questions, to let them mentor us in some important ways.

Audiences bring a much different background to the com-munication event than the relatively homogeneous people to whom I was trained to speak. The traits of *audience nouveau* are most obvious among the young, though certainly not limited to them. According to futurist Marc Prensky, before graduating from college today's youth will absorb:

- 10,000 hours playing video
- 200,000 e-mails and instant messages sent and received
- 10,000 hours talking, playing games, and using data on cell phones
- 20,000 hours watching TV
- 500,000 commercials
- 5,000 hours of book reading[2]

But these trends hardly confine themselves to Generation X and the Millennials. In the aggregate, we Americans spend two-thirds of every twelve-hour day consuming media in some form, an activity more prevalent than any other in our lives—including friendships—with adults actually somewhat *more* exposed than are teens.[3] Placing this media tidal wave in histori-cal context, marketing specialist Meg Kinney cites examples such as Columbine and September 11, stating that the Millennials uniquely have witnessed "more formative experiences in a five-year period than any other generation has experienced."[4]

To the person of a century ago, whose access to information was relatively minimal, a sermon or public lecture might have seemed like a cup of cold water in the desert. But to a listener today stuffed with hundreds of e-mails, thousands of texts, and millions of images, another talk can seem like a cup of water thrown into an ocean. Speaking in the context of marketing, Patrick Dixon, Europe's leading futurist, observes a parallel: "We will not reach this new citizen through traditional means of communication. Consider the filters we have in place to ignore the marketing information we do not want, and then consider the filtering power of a 21-year-old in 2012."⁵ This innate command of filtering power gives audience nouveau the qualities of Teflon: words don't stick.

When combined with a declining level of biblical literacy, both outsiders and insiders can find themselves hearing messages that are scripturally accurate and clearly presented but that achieve less traction in the hearer's life than the speaker realizes. One college student, for example, posted a blog titled "A Letter to the Preacher" to give future chapel speakers at his Christian university a dose of reality: "Dear, Mr. or Mrs. Chapel Speaker, When it comes to the three to five point sermons you preach. I'm sorry to say, but I find them useless. . . . I'm sorry if this brings you down. It isn't your fault you do things this way. It's natural for you, because it's what you were taught to do by professors and it's what your church expects you to do every Sunday morning."⁶

With this listener I can get the facts straight, run humorous video clips, and use language eloquently, but still miss the opportunity to influence a life because my methods are just that: mine.

I experienced the listener's plight when making the mistake of watching the second film first in the *Lord of the Rings* trilogy. Like a junior high school student cheating on a book report, I decided to skip the books and wait for the movie version, seeing no harm in diving right into the middle of the epic.

Impressive special effects and impeccable acting all failed to solve my central problem: I could not understand the story. *Rings* fans counseled and coached me, explaining characters, subplots, and the nuances of life in the shire. But all of these pieces never placed the torrent of fantasy imagery into some kind of form. Watching the third and then first movies out of sequence only made things worse.

I realized that my reaction to the trilogy must be very much the way audiences sometimes experience presentations on Christianity. They may laugh at the jokes, read Scripture from the screen on the wall, and even grasp the main point, but what is the movie about? My training assumed that audiences both depended on me as the primary interpreter of spiritual things and brought at least a modicum of biblical background to the communication event. Audience nouveau, however, may enjoy and totally relate to the story of David and Goliath but have no idea how it reveals God's love for the world through Christ's death and resurrection. Reflecting on this issue from a staff role at a major young adult magazine, Adrian observes that Millennials connect with the idea of "a common theme or symbolism running throughout Scripture. . . . Illuminating a meta-narrative gives Millennials something to attach themselves to that is much bigger than themselves. It makes them part of a movement." From Adrian's perspective, communicating a series of ideas distilled from the Bible is unlikely to mobilize younger adults unless it immerses them in the sweep of the narrative itself. Young adults I know who are giving their lives to Christian service of all kinds—from doing mission work outside their homeland to community development among the marginalized—are doing so because they bought into not an idea but the reality of the Kingdom of God announced by Jesus. It is this announcement that needs to reverberate through Christian communication, whether handling ideas, describing individual scenes, or addressing the big story directly—all of which are important in their own way. Thus, without an understanding of the big story the individual scenes, as valuable as they are, may attract and fascinate but still leave listeners of all kinds with little awareness of how they represent what Paul termed "the gospel I preached to you, which you received and on which you have taken your stand."[7] Ironically, this new discipline actually calls for better exegesis, clearer propositional thinking, and more innovative modes of presentation.

One could argue that if I had simply read the *Rings* books first, my problems would have been solved. In the same sense, Christian communicators may implicitly be demanding that listeners work on the discipline of regular Scripture reading until they are qualified to be our audience. Alternatively, I could simply watch the *Rings* films out of order long enough to piece together the plot, much as we ask listeners to hear different aspects of the big story weekly in the hope that, over time, they will put things together. Or we could just reverse things and begin listening to them.

Learning from Listeners

My favorite part of teaching a seminary course "Ministry in Emerging Culture" involved a one-hour lecture by Ellen, a bright woman in her early twenties who designed my first Website while working for a parachurch ministry in the area. Standing before students, many of whom were twice her age and with years already invested in vocational ministry, Ellen exhibited the confidence of her generation in her opening line: "If I never heard another three-point sermon in my life, I could still die happy." In the silence that ensued I enjoyed watching the blood drain from the faces of experienced preachers who had doubtless heard confessions of unspeakable sin but had never had anyone talk to them *like this*. With the shock of her initial sentence in place, Ellen proceeded to describe the Millennial generation for the mostly Boomer and Xer students, making it clear that she longed for credible alternatives to most conventional ministry forms, sermons included.

Ellen's deconstruction of my class proved much more fun than some of my own encounters over the next few years of field research among young audiences that produced these illustrations of what can be learned by listening to them.

When I Say "Lipitor," They Think "Viagra"

A seminar on preaching for a group of discipleship students at a Texas church furnished my first jarring revelation. While speaking on generational issues, I defined the Baby Boomers as "people my age who are sustained by Lipitor," only to discover that this reference, which older audiences seemed to find funny, got not a whisper of response. I did notice several students, though, swiveling their heads to look at my wife seated about half-way back in the small crowd, every time I tried to wring comedy out of Lipitor. Eating spaghetti with some of the church's staff about two hours later, Mike, who leads the young adult program, disclosed that my joke got no response because the students confused Lipitor, a cholesterol-lowering medication, with Viagra, the only drug that nightly television ads taught them to associate with aging Boomers. I realized that although words are in the public domain their meanings are not, and so I began experimenting with speaking from manuscripts to gain greater control over word choice and even create the option of asking an audience member to review talks in advance.

When I Say "My Third Point Is . . ." They Think "When Is This Going to Be Over?"

Several young people have shared with me the value of a speaker who "keeps your attention the entire time, not just in the beginning." One focus group of Texas students expressed the strong sentiment that "anything more than thirty minutes is too long and we fall asleep," and eighteen-year-old Karen was very clear that the length of a talk did not matter to her as long as "it is good," defined by another student as entertaining, engaging, and easy to follow. I sensed that entertainment led to engagement, which in turn produced ease of following along.

Many focus groups, for example, have reported that being "interesting" is the primary trait of a great sermon or teaching. One student defined this characteristic by citing the example of a favorite speaker ("His stuff is very original . . . stuff you wouldn't think of yourself") and conversely noting that a poor presentation usually included the kind of material she could have just read at home. In other words, if I am not engaging and original, *everyone* has a short attention span. I began to think of these listeners as all holding remote controls in their hands ready to surf to another mental channel the instant I stopped engaging them. I decided in response to adopt a twenty-five-minute limit for presentations to Millennials and then expanded the policy to all large group settings that permit it. The limit is reinforced by the most valuable piece of hardware I own: a digital count-down timer from Radio Shack.

When I Say "In the Original Greek . . ." They Think "Tell Me Why That Matters"

I received a rude introduction to this kind of thinking when a student raised his hand during a lecture at a small New England college and asked me bluntly, "Why do we need to know this stuff?" I am morally certain he spoke for the rest of the class that day. This challenge captures the young adult definition of the word *relevant*. As one focus group described it, a presentation with this trait deals with "things that are applicable, things that leave you with a reasonable challenge, something that inspires passion, something that's convincing with evidence to back up what you say, something that really speaks to a need." Another person added, "It applies to your life and it, like, impacts you." More specifically, twenty-one-year-old Kara related her great respect for the sermons of her church's young adult pastor because his talks were "very down to earth."

Earning a hearing with audience nouveau means presenting talks that are a paradox: they envelop the most practical aspects of living within the cosmic metanarrative, the big story of God's redemptive activity as depicted in scripture, without being either mystical or formulaic. There are easier alternatives. Talking one day with an experienced youth conference speaker, I took the opportunity to ask him how to preach to teens, something I had never done. He replied that only one thing was really necessary: rewrite your sermons to put "Teenager!" at the beginning of each declarative sentence. So simply replace, "You need to draw close to God," with, "Teenager! You need to draw close to God." Years later, I revealed this trade secret to a group of several hundred teens during a talk. They laughed in derision. I started focusing more on challenging them to believe that the big story of the Scriptures changes everything if we become part of it, rather than just inviting God to become a part of our story.

When I Say "George Barna Reported . . ." They Think "OK, but Who Are You?"

The classic feature of audience nouveau is the insistence on *authenticity*. Boomers tend to see this trait as a self-deprecating platform persona who tells a few jokes at her or his own expense. The young adults I have met appreciate the humor but despise the idea of the persona. Kara, for example, disdained Christian communicators who put on their "speaker self." In her mind, being real involved qualities much more important than being eloquent. Another group of young leaders made the point more specific: "A lot of times preachers will just say things but won't give you the story of how they have changed." In other words, if the message hasn't helped me personally, how can I expect to make the case that it can help them?

If I don't open up my life, I mean *really* open it up, a message can seem *true but unreal* to an audience that requires both. As one focus group stated, an authentic communicator is one with "no front or mask." The college student who wrote to future chapel speakers offers them a prescription. "Do you get what I'm saying? Tell me about what has gone on in your life. Tell me how the 'Living Word' is living, or be honest and tell me how it isn't living in your life. I want to know more about you yourself, not the Greek or Hebrew, or hermeneutical techniques you learned in your studies. Give me yourself, the struggles, the triumphs, the frustrations. The joy; these are the things I can relate to. . . . In fact, I highly respect your willingness to be vulnerable about your spiritual journey."[8]

This undergraduate with the nerve to advise nationally known public speakers captures the sentiment of an emerging generation that respects age but despises pretense. As Karen put it, communicators need to be honest and direct, not trying to "cover up the truth." In fact, the marketing firm Integer reports that when young adult males are asked about the type of celebrities they admire, they tend to show the greatest respect for those termed "talented authentics" who combine honesty and accessibility with the ability to get the job done while being true to themselves.[9] Without all of these traits, a talk sounds to Kara like something "I could have just read . . . 'here's the facts.'"

When I Say "Let Me Illustrate That for You," They Think "Don't Just Tell Me, Involve Me"

The young people Janet and I know strongly prefer active participation to passive reception, saying the services they remember most "were those that we were a part of." One young woman told us, for example, that a good communicator "must get me emotionally involved . . . I just need the rollercoaster." Another commented that this connection takes root best when speakers spend time with young adults outside the presentation, citing

Mike's practice of playing basketball with young people at retreat events and his well-known ability to remember names. Also, media such as video clips, which seem passive to me, actually encourage their sense of involvement by couching the message in their native grammar (images on screen) in a way that stimulates lots of reaction (that is, laughter). But complex methods are not necessary. The precise way that involvement is achieved (dialogue, tech, prayer, and so on) is much less important than the opportunity to partner with us in creating the experience.

Looking for ways to open avenues of participation I started experimenting with the idea, borrowed from my friend Sam Farina, of asking audiences to send me text messages during my talks. In one case, the purpose was to generate data for debriefing afterwards, but in other situations I ask for questions that I promise to read aloud and respond to at intervals during the presentation. As with Lipitor, I find that what I am saying and what they are thinking about are often strikingly mismatched, but the gesture of inclusion opens a dialogue through which I communicate with them and they mentor me. The effect does not depend on receiving profound messages. During one presentation to a young adult group, Jan and I received texts containing theological questions such as why God allows evil, fashion questions about skincare, and cultural concerns such as what sorts of music we like. But that day, the largest share of the messages focused on asking us what mistakes we had made in our lives and what we would do differently. The connection we felt with this group did not result from our brilliant answers but from our willingness to discuss anything, and to do so using a medium native to Millennials. Using their questions put the discussion on their terms.

The Transformers

Even though audience nouveau possesses many traits in common with all American audiences, they also have their own pronounced tendencies. These qualities are not destiny, but understanding them can help older communicators translate their messages into forms that meet the definition of effectiveness given to me by one young person: "Whenever you feel sad that that person is done talking." In other words, even audience nouveau can be so moved by a talk that they are sorry to see it end.

Some time ago I attended a special preview showing of the *Transformers* movie at the invitation of a group of students from our seminary, one of whom, Jordan, even bought my ticket. Having grown up watching *Superman* in black and white, I was almost totally ignorant of the robot-as-Swiss Army knife plot at the heart of this action science fiction film. But the mostly twenty- and thirtysomething crowd that packed the darkness around me did have these memories. Unaware that the film whose preview was about to begin would make a million dollars an hour on its first day, I started interviewing Ryan and Joel, the two students seated on either side of me, about just exactly what we had come to the theater to see.

With their background briefing in place, the lights came down and I watched several hundred people sitting in rows not unlike pews cross over into another world for two hours. Some of this effect doubtless stemmed from their childhood devotion to the storyline, reinforced by endless comics, toys, and television programs. Now, with the help of millions of dollars in computer-generated imagery, fictional alien robots transformed them, inviting the audience not just into suspension of disbelief but into becoming temporary citizens of an alternative reality.

Driving home from the theater, I reflected on how seldom it is that speaking (including my own) exerts this effect on listeners. Announcing the arrival of the Kingdom of God offers a new reality like no other, yet a lot of our communication about it takes the form of lists of ideas about God, outlines of the Bible, solutions for our problems, poems, or very long stories. All of these are fine, and all have their place, but none of them makes me feel like the people in that theater felt.

I used to think that making my communication more "visual" by using slides or video clips was the answer given the postmodern prioritization of media by young adults. As useful as this approach can be, something much more is involved: the feeling of being gripped by the transcendent. The visual is mainly present by coincidence. Perhaps this explains why preachers using video are delivering messages all over the country with no more effect than their prevideo sermons.

I have to believe that hearing Jesus speak must have touched people in this transcendent way. He perplexed them by using parables few could understand. He baffled them by posing questions instead of answers. He amazed them with signs and wonders. Everything he did suggested the in-breaking of a reality beyond anything imagined in ancient Palestine (or contemporary America). His crucifixion and resurrection were the ultimate prediction of what became possible in this new world.

The theater audience was caught up in a powerful, but temporary, experience during the preview. They illustrated for me that something more than creativity and nonlinear thinking supported by video is possible when Christians speak. If we listen to audience nouveau long enough, allowing them to be our mentors, perhaps we can learn how to communicate the big story in a way that makes it not just true but more real than anything else.

9

LEADERSHIP

Learning from Followers

I listened quietly as the group of young leaders around me ate designer salads and poured out a litany of concerns about their even younger charges. Accustomed to conversations in which Gen Xers complain about Boomers or Boomers disparage Xers, I found myself unprepared for what I heard from a group of leaders half my age recounting their struggles in leading a ministry composed of even younger adults. With much head-shaking and eye-rolling, they recounted stories of trying to direct students involved in a discipleship program designed especially for "Twixters," so called because they were between high school and the onset of full-on adult life. They loved their students very much, but these young leaders struggled with the overprotective mothers and fathers who were now known as "helicopter" parents because of their hovering ways. They also told of a seeming immunity to instruction, meaning that the same student who could hack into Amazon could not find a can of paint at Wal-Mart after extensive coaching and repeated cell phone calls from the store. "They don't know how to use a screwdriver," one staffer lamented, while another pointed out that the selectivity of the students' attention was so finely tuned to humorous videos and things "about me" that little else made it through their filters.

Although our dialogue over lunch probably included issues leaders have been discussing since the tower of Babel ("What's the matter with kids these days?"), it also offered some confirmation of an urban legend: that the Boomer versus Builder or even Boomer versus Xer generation gap may pale in comparison to the fault line growing between Generation X and the Millennials. Some cultural differences between the groups are obvious. For example, many regard the television series *Beverly Hills 90210,* which premiered in 1990, as the first fully Gen X program. The equivalent for Millennials would be *Dawson's Creek,* which was not even in the top twenty-five of the shows most watched by Xers.[1] In fact, only two animated programs on Fox, *The Simpsons* and *Family Guy,* appear in the top ten most viewed programs for both groups.[2] Apart from a mutual affection for Bart Simpson, then, these two cohorts, like their older peers, could find that their different cultural assumptions and formative experiences make leadership situations frustrating as the natives of Beverly Hills 90210 try to lead the citizens of Dawson's Creek.

A small survey project even finds the two groups quite distinct on ten of sixteen personality traits.[3] Unlike a person my age, to whom everyone under forty seems "young," as these tribes encounter each other in ministry and for-profit leadership situations sensitivity to their other dissimilarities appears to be growing. Talking with the frustrated leadership team at lunch that day, I presented them with a challenge that parallels the focus of this chapter: do not start changing your leadership until you have listened to those expected to follow. I sensed that their young adult program, largely designed for and operated by their 90210 generation might have less traction with the natives of Dawson's Creek who came to the experience from a different generational culture. Forcing the latter group to immigrate to the 90210 territory was asking them to become what they were not. Finding out how to lead them means asking them about that, placing them in the reverse mentor role.

Power Is Ignorance

In an earlier chapter, we discussed how power brings with it special forms of blindness. However, climbing the power curve also raises the difficulty of climbing the learning curve; that is, the more influence and information I possess as a leader, the less I may actually know about how to lead. Sitting in the coffee shop of a large, nationally franchised bookstore, I enjoyed the opportunity to overhear a conversation among several bored college-age employees standing behind the counter where I had just ordered my drink. They laughed out loud not at a joke but at a recent directive from senior management that had become a joke to them. After serious deliberation, corporate leadership decided that, regardless of one's function in their bookstores, each employee needed to live by the mantra, "We are all booksellers." The twentysomethings tasked with making cappuccinos found this hysterical, mocking the phrase by comparing it to their actual daily tasks: squirting steamed milk into designer drinks, selling the occasional pastry, and refilling air pots. Clearly feeling more in common with Starbucks than with Gutenberg, they executed these functions only a few feet from stacks of books but felt this made them booksellers only in the sense that a trip to the airport made them pilots. Their reaction sparked an image in my mind: somewhere, perhaps in a corner office overlooking a Mercedes parked below, sat the vice president responsible for this bold innovation, totally unaware that her or his followers experienced the new directive only as stinging irony, a joke imposed at their expense. They did *not* sell books; they poured coffee into paper cups. Whatever information formed the company's new slogan (most likely massive amounts of research) actually cultivated *ignorance* among its leaders, who confused their reality with that of the much younger employees who had no input into or ownership of the process.

Michael Useem, professor of management at the Wharton School, states pointedly that "there's no gene for management, there's no gene for leadership. They simply have to be learned."[4] The discipline of reverse mentoring assumes that these skills also need to be *relearned* regularly from unlikely sources such as those who follow us. Even though the young change our world every day in technological and cultural revolutions, organizational leaders in this context can find themselves overinformed but underenlightened. Some of the obstacles to learning, such as ego protection, cultural barriers between generations, or the sense of entitlement that naturally accompanies age and experience, probably inhere in all forms of human activity. (Today's hip young leader may be tomorrow's change resister, for example.) But certain forms of learning resistance seem especially acute for ministry leaders.

Comfortable Ignorance

Management thought leader Tom Peters, himself having publicly abandoned many of the ideas presented in his groundbreaking 1983 book *In Search of Excellence*, cites the pressing necessity of *unlearning* things we assumed to be true. This aptitude proves difficult for all leaders but is especially challenging for nonprofits such as ministry organizations. While the rest of the world, says Peters, is "experimenting like crazy with radical stuff," nonprofits tend to be reactive to trends because their leaders reflect the opinions of their most influential and conservative members. He describes these leaders and their organizations (in typical Peters style) as "doomed."[5] Although the verdict seems extreme, the validity of his premise commands attention. To maintain their base of resources and support, ministry leaders face the unspoken pressure to mold their philosophy and practice around the preferences of those who supply these assets.

Steve, a church planter in a suburban area, for example, told me of painful conflicts over his lack of the "big personality" leadership style and insider focus that many of his previously churched members demanded. He felt the temptation to spin the ministry's ethos subtly in the direction that would appeal to these people because they controlled most of the financial assets. (If you don't think that's possible, ask yourself what your ministry would look like if the majority of its financial support came from people under twenty-five, or an ethnic group other than your own.) The possible benefits of Steve's compliance included the loyal support of his transfer members and the ability to feed his family. But the penalties involved alienating outsiders who exhibited an unswerving distaste for the celebrity model of leadership they regarded as an exercise in narcissism at best, or a triumph of authoritarianism at worst.

Steve chose the penalties associated with maintaining the congregation's missional focus on the unchurched and paid the price. He simply allowed his rechurched people to decide whether or not to join in this journey. Some did. Some did not. Steve would resist the comparison, but I could not help thinking of the description of Moses in Hebrews, as he who "regarded disgrace for the sake of Christ as of greater value than the treasures of Egypt."[6] Of course, the same conflict might arise in the opposite direction (a ministry chasing trends, or overly focused on outsiders), but my travels in this decade have not turned up many exemplars. The kind of ignorance of the outside world that Peters describes seems much more prevalent, with courageous leaders like Steve insisting that the comforting thing to know isn't always the right thing to know.

Trained Ignorance

A second obstacle to learning actually derives its power from the techniques we use to acquire knowledge. The adage that information is power contains enough truth to suggest the converse: that power is information—in other words, achieving the level of influence I need or desire brings with it access to information unavailable at lower power levels. My doctoral students, for example, sometimes come to their first course expecting me to identify books or present lectures that contain the hitherto secret knowledge they need if they are to achieve real leadership excellence. Many mature leaders (themselves now in the upline position) who buy this premise tend to trust in massive doses of information to solve the problems of their followers and organizations. Missiologist Alan Johnson, for instance, discovered a pattern in ministry leadership training during field research in Asia. He observed that diligent application of various courses and resources for shaping disciples and developing leaders repeatedly produced disappointing results. Though students grasped some new material, many failed to exhibit enough new behavior to justify the effort. This realization invariably led to a search for new and better curricula, which, applied with the same diligence, produced about the same results, leading to yet another search for better materials.[7]

American organizations often exhibit a variant of the same trait. One survey of human resources professionals, for example, finds 83 percent of them recommending more training as the basic strategy for increasing worker productivity, a model critics describe as depending on "static, classroom-delivered content that is already months out of date before the room of students are forced into attendance."[8] Johnson concludes that the issue of curriculum, although significant, matters far less than the fact that the leadership-training model originated in another context altogether and consequently operates on faulty cultural assumptions. Conventional ministry training, with all of its positive features, can do just as much to cultivate ignorance by giving us the illusion that we know what matters when we do not.

Learning from those we intend to lead offers a way to escape our own perspective (a grace the bookstore's management lacked) and change not just our curriculum but our basic approach to leading. As part of a conference at a small Christian college, for instance, my friend Rusty, the campus pastor, invited our group to join an informal "chapel" service of about seventy-five students meeting around tables in the cafeteria. We took the opportunity to mix my mostly older folk in with small groups of students to discuss the issue of passing the leadership baton from one generation to another. A debrief later on revealed that almost everyone had a very positive experience, with many mentions of the need to give younger leaders a chance, and the potential impact of reverse mentoring, and the priority of passing the baton from one generation to the next.

However, my own experience went in another direction. Just before we formed our discussion groups, I interviewed Andrew, a student leader, about the kinds of questions we should ask on a subject I thought I knew inside and out. I felt quite clever taking the time to preview the discussion items with a native of young adult culture, until he asked me, "Why would we *want* the baton you are passing to us?" He went on to illustrate his point with the example of his peers who were already forming or joining start-up companies with no intention of waiting around for Boomers to give them opportunities within a system that always gave them home field advantage. That hurt. In many hours of writing and talking about baton passing, I had assumed the whole time that we had something younger leaders *wanted* to inherit. But what if it's not true? What if the whole idea of a baton passing from older to younger implies that oldsters hold all the assets in the relationship and have the divine right to decide who receives what, making them the gatekeepers of the future? Although older leaders can indeed help the young find their calling in some important ways, Andrew questioned the attitude with which they offer guidance, implying "I'll give you the baton if you promise to do things my way."

Kristin, another undergraduate, put a fine edge on the issue by telling our debriefing session the real problem she heard during the discussions was just fear. The old are afraid of letting go, the young are afraid of making mistakes, and neither side is trusting Jesus to be head of the church and guide everyone involved. Kristin's comments dropped a bomb in the room. Really, if we were trusting God, would people my age hold on so tight, and would it be so difficult to find church planters? Kristin, Andrew, and their peers delivered me from my own well-informed perspective on that Friday, one that assumed a certain receptivity on the part of the young.

The discomfort of finding that my assumption was defective helped me unlearn, and it implied that leading these followers requires a commitment to the principle that the "baton" symbolizes the gospel as expressed in the mission of the church but not necessarily in its institutions. "We have this treasure," Paul writes, "in jars of clay to show that this all-surpassing power is from God and not from us."[9] Learning from the proven character and the life experience of older people can offer great value to the young, but these assets are transmitted through relationship and example, not by a hand-off. Followers will respond to the influence of those devoted to the treasure rather than to the clay jars.

Ignorance Is Power

In some critical ways, no one knows *less* than the person in charge until that person allows followers to suggest a new set of assumptions for their context. Simple power distance puts initiative on this issue in the hands of the leader; few followers will risk pointing out the boss's deficiencies in order to extend their services as a reverse mentor. Ironically, then, the very people who could do us the most good often feel the most unable to speak to us because no invitation is forthcoming. R-mentoring formalizes the invitation into a relationship that draws out the primary asset of people without position and experience: what they do *not* know. Guy Kawasaki surmises that proven people "don't admit what they don't know, but assume they know everything . . . [while unproven people] don't know what they don't know, so they're willing to try anything. . . . Ignorance is not only bliss, it's empowering."[10] The challenge for those who guide a ministry of any kind is the realization that no one sees things more clearly than the inexperienced person who remains (albeit briefly) *organizationally naïve*.

In this connection, some ministries now use a variety of contact strategies, among them a growing number of Web-based reviews, to assimilate the views of visitors and new members into their planning.

However, the power that ignorance supplies also resides within not-so-new people who will respond to a leadership style that empowers them to see the ministry in a new way. I encountered one example of this dynamic in the same coffee-house conversation with Steve, my church planter friend. After several years of focusing the ministry and building trust with the people, he pulled the core leadership together to ask them (and himself) a defining question about their life together: "Is this the church we dreamed of being?" That one question kicked off a series of what he calls "structured conversations" about the future, conversations that put everything on the table—including his role as the senior leader—in an open forum. For example, even though their stated goal of delivering "church for the unchurched" remained the same, Steve wanted to know whether this statement expressed a reality or just a slogan. "We need to be OK inviting people into community who make us really uncomfortable being in community," he maintained. Stretching over several months, these ongoing talks led to the gratifying personal realization that Steve's leadership team supported him and that he genuinely liked them. These sometimes painful discussions also yielded strategic decisions that would shape the congregation's future in critical ways. For example, the leaders made the commitment *not* to buy a building—ever—in order to avoid siphoning off resources and attention to a facility when those assets could be better invested reaching out to their community.

Steve's key leaders knew a great deal about all of their church's operations and so could not be thought of as organizationally naïve. With enough of the "hard conversations" behind him to have established real trust and ownership, however, Steve's leadership brought out a *collaborative naiveté*. His willingness to put his own job at risk in order to ask that first fateful question created the very real opportunity to forge a future through cooperation. In this context, the leadership arrived at a new vantage point from which they could evaluate their present with ruthless honesty and visualize tomorrow with sincere faith. Rather than dominating the proceedings, in this situation Steve simply facilitated the process of interaction by using what he regards as one of his primary gifts: "leading from the middle." Those who insist on leading from the top in every situation may find the collaborative naiveté in short supply within their ministries and remain informed but unenlightened.

Banks and Campuses

Working in a large bank during a recession, I spent each day in a group of several dozen temporary staff members, all subemployed after layoffs from their real jobs elsewhere in the city. The tense atmosphere was punctuated by shouting, some of it by the staff directed through telephones at customers with overdue payments, and the rest of it in the form of tirades from Jim, our manager. He spent most of his day out of sight in an office, emerging to check on things and deliver an occasional harangue, often after meeting with Eric, his rather grim immediate superior.

The institution's answer to its financial woes took the form of one of the quality assurance programs popular at the time, the logo of which appeared on posters, brochures, and even coffee mugs. Someone in management apparently believed that these promotional items held the power to erase our awareness of the recession and our doubts about ever landing a decent job somewhere else, so that our entire loyalty would be devoted to excellence in banking—at five to seven dollars an hour.

The crowning moment of my sojourn through quality assurance arrived one morning along with the smell of bacon and eggs. Jim informed us, in a normal voice this time, of a breakfast buffet being served in an upstairs hallway to which we were all invited in just a few minutes. Walking upstairs to the narrow, linoleum corridor, the staff found Jim and Eric in white paper chef's hats manning stainless steel tubs of food. We piled breakfast onto paper plates quickly, because the "chefs" had informed us that the meal was to be eaten back downstairs as we worked at our desks.

The bank made a massive investment in training its staff and aligning its processes with their quality model, only to leave its lowest-paid employees eating scrambled eggs at their workstations as managers unwittingly mocked themselves by wearing the white paper hat of someone who serves. As with the bookstore leadership mentioned earlier, the bank's management trained itself into ignorance, becoming less able to lead with each new application of training for its employees. Information obscured enlightenment because it remained trapped inside management's frame of reference, a point of view dominated by the sorts of fears that bad economic times tend to produce and hierarchical leadership tends to accentuate. Having real-world experience, but lacking any organizational power, the employees were trapped inside management's frame of reference, with its fear that they would use any excuse to fail to perform, leaving the workers with little hope of escaping until the recession ended.

Learning from followers lances our inappropriate leadership assumptions with the sharp truths only followers possess, offering the possibility of changing how we do things in important ways. One large corporation illustrated this kind of logic by supplementing its professional R&D staff of seven thousand with a network of nonemployee amateurs potentially numbering in the millions. The model has already produced several major new product lines in an attempt eventually to develop half of their new products using this "Pro-Am" concept.[11] Speaking in the context of nonprofits breaking out of their organizational ignorance by drawing on the young, Peters argues that these organizations face oblivion if "at least 25 percent of your board is not under the age of 29."[12] Although the claim may seem radical, the principle of learning from followers remains valid, with some companies implementing systems such as 360-degree review, in which leaders receive evaluation not just from upline managers but also from their own reports. No one knows more about my leadership than the people who have to follow it.

The early church demonstrated this same wisdom by resolving the controversy over the care of Greek versus Hebrew speaking widows by asking the believers in Jerusalem themselves to nominate the leadership who would straighten things out, a proposal that "pleased the whole group."[13] Regardless of the example, biblical, corporate, or ministry, the principle remains that leaders who listen to followers using practices such as reverse mentoring will have the best chance of leading them appropriately and collaborating to accomplish ministry goals that matter. Sam and Laura, for example, leaders of a collegiate ministry, told me of their decision to split their large worship service into three separate experiences, essentially creating a multisite ministry on one campus. Having built the group up to an attendance in the hundreds, and being highly regarded by their peers, they simply felt that something had to change in the ministry they had known for more than fifteen years. They realized that "most of our fruitfulness wasn't from the way we are now, but the way we were five or six years ago when we were still hungry." The shift of ministry models proved to be one of the greatest challenges of their careers, with many times of wondering what they had gotten themselves into. But things began to change. "We realized," Laura said, "that it had been a long time since we had had eighteen-year-olds in our house." The new way of organizing ministry put them in direct contact with a much smaller group of students and thus much closer to the realities that are easily obscured in a larger group setting. The students responded so positively that Sam had to build a deck on their home to accommodate the crush of undergraduates who were now a regular feature there.

Even though the long-term future of the multisite approach is still in play, Sam and Laura told me of learning much more about themselves than they did about ministry. The challenge of working on a smaller scale again has helped to reconnect them with the realities of student life, the whole reason they got into this in the first place. Many factors contributed to their situation, but again, being up close to those who follow became an indispensable part of Sam and Laura's journey, some of the fruit of which appeared in water baptism services and other forms. Although no one would say that students taught them these things in a formal sense, simply becoming resensitized to the world of the eighteen-year-old changes what it means to be in ministry to them. A similar change would be a great benefit to so many leaders who were young just yesterday.

Part Four

DEVELOPING RECIPROCITY

10

PROTÉGÉS

Developing R-Mentoring Relationships

I few years ago I described my work with different generations of leaders as "worldview therapy," defined as anger management for the young and grief recovery for the old. Thinking I had this kind of thing pretty much sorted out, I encouraged the young to look past their anger to some new sense of mission, and for the old that their best days could still be ahead if they listened for God's voice. Bobby Welch, president of the Southern Baptist Convention, characterized the possibilities: "There are two roads to the same dream. One road is traveled by older folks who have gotten near the end of their ministries and never got to where they envisioned themselves going. They are disappointed and feel like they've failed. They are hungry for one more shot for giving their best for the rest of their lives. The other road is traveled by younger folks who are looking for something to give the rest of their lives to."[1]

Despite the cynicism or despair involved in my conversations, I never lost hope that, in Welch's terms, reconciling young leaders looking for a cause together with older leaders looking for an opportunity might give God a chance to change everyone.

Then things began to change in my communication with both tribes. First, a group of youth ministers at a retreat shocked me with their positive statements about their senior pastors. They expressed not just loyalty but love and admiration for the Boomers leading them. Didn't they know that I frequently cited this very relationship as a case study in intergenerational tension? Just weeks before, a midlife ministry leader admired by his peers confessed in front of a discussion group: "I am so tired of church." His comments took the air out of the room but found an echo in another pastor who asked me rhetorically whether he really wanted to spend his life in meetings to decide how many video surveillance cameras the nursery needed. The representativeness of these examples defies exact measurement, but they certainly suggest that at least some generational tensions are easing. Perhaps the Xers entering the midlife season that their Boomer leaders are already navigating have more in common than they realize.

A second change in my conversations involved a brand new discussion of the Millennial generation, who, outnumbering their own parents, have millions of representatives in their twenties feeling ready to lead right now. The sheer size of their cohort makes our population bimodal, with Boomers on one end of the age spectrum and Millennials on the other, and a relatively small Gen X cohort in between. Tapscott, Ticoll, and Lowry of the Alliance for Converging Technology characterize the generation as "exceptionally curious, self-reliant, contrarian, smart, focused, able to adapt, high in self-esteem, and globally oriented. These attributes, combined with [their] ease with digital tools, should threaten and challenge the traditional manager and traditional approaches to strategy. This generation will create a push for radical changes in existing companies and established institutions. . . . Their first point of reference is the Net."[2]

Adding this new variable to the generational equation immediately made everything more complex. The Builder-Boomer-Buster scenario I had relied on now seemed dated and inadequate. Yesterday's twenty-five-year-old Gen X youth pastor serves as today's forty-year-old senior pastor balancing the need to lead both the Boomers on the board and the Millennials running the youth ministry.

The surprising (to me) softening of some Boomer-Xer tensions paralleled by the arrival of new challenges for both groups in the form of the Millennials suggests an important opportunity to use reverse mentoring to form what missiologists refer to as a "third culture," a jointly fabricated space where members of two dissimilar cultures meet to begin learning to communicate. Humility and urgency are the adhesives for holding this third culture together. The questions asked by older leaders about this possibility generally come down to, "How do I get started?" This chapter deals with the practical side of finding and cultivating reverse mentoring relationships, a special form of cross-cultural friendship the very unlikeliness of which softens hearts and grows leaders.

Reverse Mentoring Relationships

The corporate experience with R-mentoring, as well as that of ministry colleagues, supports the idea that *friendship* is the core dynamic. The world produced more than 160 billion gigabytes of information in 2006 (equivalent to all the books ever written—multiplied by three million).[3] Undoubtedly, much of this data holds great significance, but something of value also resides in another form: human beings. The ultimate revelation of God comes to us in the person of Christ, rejected by many of his culture's insiders but embraced by its outsiders. Similarly, transforming wisdom comes to us through surprising, unlikely people if we possess the humility to lay aside our own expertise long enough to embrace the relationship. I cannot call you "mentor" until I have called you "friend."

Assuming I can say "I'm not cool," "I'm not relevant," and "I don't get it" (or their functional equivalents) out loud, these healthy RM friendships display certain regular features.

Surprise

A small group of young adults invited me one evening to join them for a dinner of Subway sandwiches in a convenience

store before they returned for the evening session of the conference we were all attending. Averaging perhaps nineteen years
of age, they expressed the communal customs of their tribe by
refusing to let me eat alone. I felt awkward (Boomer culture is
more individualistic) but joined them anyway at the yellow
Formica booth bolted to the floor beside the store's front window. Eating my sandwich, I listened to them describe something new: the other side of Millennial life. Their narrative
communication style generated stories of heartbreaking failure,
painful rejection, stunted aspirations, and persecution by other
Millennials—not for being Christians so much as just for being
distinct. These anecdotes added up to a photographic negative
of the way experts usually describe their generation. Instead of
sparkling with motivation and hungering for success, these three
young people sounded downcast, even a little desperate, with the
sense that most of their friends in the world were probably right
there sitting in that convenience store booth at the moment.
Millennial stereotypes, then, even though perhaps generally
accurate, may derive so much of their content from the highly
nurtured, college-bound, upwardly mobile young adults that the
generation's struggles remain in the shadows.

My three-person faculty delivered an unexpected lesson that
evening on the difference between portraying a group and reduc-
ing it to a bulleted list of traits that render some of its members invisible. Working from the protégé role with R-mentors,
then, requires shock-absorbing grace to lessen the impact of
the unforeseen. The search for that grace encourages the kind
of humility that acts as both the cause and the effect of reverse
mentoring. The primary attribute of this humility consists of *not
reacting* when a comment reveals our limitations, or an observation discloses our ignorance, or the R-mentor's example implicitly questions mine. Stifling the natural tendency to debate,
disagree, or try to trump the R-mentor's thoughts with our own
is essential to preserving the integrity of the process and the
humility so crucial to its power.

Variety

Reverse mentoring opportunities present themselves in diverse formats. Actually, the conventional understanding of the word *mentor* as a more experienced person who imparts knowledge to the less experienced describes most of my R-mentoring relationships. Experimenting with another form, I asked Dave, a cultural informant, to round up a group of his fellow youth pastors for an interview at a downtown coffeehouse. With a pledge of anonymity in place, and plied with liberal doses of French press coffee, they began to tell me of the secret world of the American youth pastor. Their candid self-disclosure provoked more than research conclusions, confronting me inadvertently with how my own leadership had failed youth pastors who worked for me. The group's format lent an inescapable credibility to both their story and its implications for senior pastors.

Most R-mentoring probably takes place in a person-to-person (P2P) model, with small groups representing the second most common approach, but the practice finds its way into other forms as well. Triads, for example, in which two people—sometimes a married couple—work with one protégé (P22P, person-to-two-people) also offer some valuable dynamics. Interviewing Sonia and Peter on the attitudes of young Pentecostal leaders toward their tradition, I found that the triad format allowed my R-mentors to interact with each other *while* they were interacting with me, supporting refinement of their insights and enriching my understanding with nuances unlikely to come from just one person. As Sonia spoke, Peter supplied examples or suggested alternative ways of looking at things. Sonia did the same for him as I, listening to them both, learned more from their interactions at times than from my own questions. This simple feature, of course, benefits the protégé in any format involving more than a sole R-mentor, so long as group interaction remains possible.

However, learning is also available in far larger groups. Looking over fifty text messages sent in by several hundred college students during a talk, I felt proud of myself for using (actually copying) an edgy method. A group of about a dozen Gen X leaders helped me debrief the next day, searching for the implications of these messages and producing a fascinating exhibition of thirty-year-olds struggling to understand twenty-year-olds. As usual, the struggle yielded some surprises for all of us:

- *Style:* There were many more texts about my new hipster glasses than about Jesus. "The glasses should stay. It takes the focus off your bald spot," one message recommended.
- *Peers:* The cryptic texts plainly conveyed the idea that we were peers. "Hey, Earl. I have funky glasses too," one student remarked, "That means we're both fabulous."

This MP2P (many-people-to-person) encounter revealed that their assumptions about communication seemed to be modeled after the Internet, where connectivity tends to be multiple, simultaneous, and lateral. Confrontation, then, seemed not to offend them at all so long as I never used it to imply a superior position. The MP2P format, amenable to many methods other than texting, offered the vibe, the scale, and the anonymity that produced genuine insight.

Depth

Like friendships in general, R-mentoring takes place on many levels of interpersonal bonding and over many intervals of time. Important learnings result from both profound, long-term relationships with R-mentors who become lifetime friends and brief, one-time conversations with the person next to us on an airplane, and from every possible variant in between. I think of the shallower, short-term form of RM as the "tech support" model in which, for example, I e-mail a younger friend, as I did today, asking why my Word documents do not attach properly to my e-mails. My mentor and I may enjoy a very meaningful friendship on other grounds, but these requests only accompany it; they do not create it. On the other end of the scale, protégés who begin with a simple request for a solution or insight find themselves, over time, developing the kind of vulnerability required to grow into long-term confidants. I continue to benefit from mentors of both kinds.

Growing as a leader takes many forms and happens in many ways, some as simple as applying a new technology and others as profound as searing repentance and reconciliation. R-mentoring offers one vehicle flexible enough to accommodate learning and transformation in multiple forms. Potential protégés need to realize that attempting to fit these relationships into a one-size-fits-all mold demonstrates exactly the attitude that RM specializes in undoing. Allowing each mentoring connection to find its own level offers a more organic and productive approach to the discipline because it allows my mentors to specialize in *their* giftedness rather than in my preferences. Along the way, protégés benefit from the ability to draw on multiple R-mentors at varying times and in varying combinations to bring the full diversity of the body of Christ to their aid, "so that there should be no division in the body, but that its parts should have equal concern for each other."[4] Shared concern helps form the third culture in which R-mentoring operates.

The huge variety of R-mentoring formats can be depicted in a simple diagram placing the diversity dimension into relationship with the depth dimension. Most of the commonly used models can be located somewhere within the territory defined by the intersection of these two traits.

For purposes of clarity, this diagram casts these dimensions as polar opposites (they are not) and excludes the variety of communication channels through which R-mentoring flows (ranging from in-person to the Internet). The point of the enterprise is to encourage the new protégé to take full advantage of the many paths forward that RM offers, as well as to explore new ways of employing the practice. The closer a leader comes to the confidant end of the scale, the greater the potential for profound change; but great benefits can also accrue in every other form of this discipline, often when we least expect it.

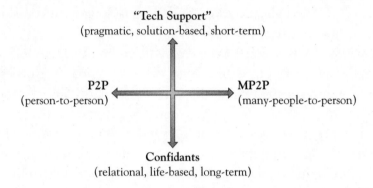

Reverse Mentoring Best Practices

Saying "I am not cool," "I'm not relevant," and "I don't get it" starts the RM process, to which the young can respond, "I respect that," "I can help," and most of all "I'll be you one day." This kind of vulnerability is the Esperanto, the contrived but common language of reverse mentoring; it offers not a cure for generational tension but a way of preventing these natural struggles from squandering our potential together.

This potential develops through a simple process of building respect and trust using certain common ingredients.

Believing

Without faith that God could use this practice in an important way, no mere technique will change a leader into a protégé. Evading these relationships is just too appealing to the part of us that exults in status. However, simple trust that God moves when we humble ourselves positions us both to find R-mentors by design and to embrace the "accidental" learning experiences that often are the most fruitful variety. In fact, the gap between generations is not always as wide as we think. In one survey, three-fourths of workers over fifty-five reported that they relate well to their younger co-workers, with 43 percent saying they learned from them. About half of younger workers (eighteen to thirty-four) reported they got along well with their older peers, while almost two-thirds claim to have learned from them.[5] Market research and employee surveys hardly constitute a substitute for faith, but they do help to deflate our doubts about the potential for spiritual reconciliation leading to intergenerational collaboration.

Choosing

Most of my R-mentoring relationships started as a "sacred accident," a surprising intervention that somehow turned out to accomplish God's purposes. On more than one occasion, a chance meeting in a hotel lobby or an invitation for late-night coffee with a small group changed my attitude, broadened my understanding, or offered the best form of rebuke: the unintentional kind. As the next chapter illustrates, sometimes the people involved sought me out, but even then the original plan never really included my serving in the protégé role; that came later. After a long chain of these seeming accidents, many of them starting with a small request for technical help, it was a pattern of learning, change, and enjoyment that appeared, encouraging me to begin serving as a protégé by design. As many corporations have done, I started with the issue of technology, getting help from young people like Kevin and Glen, generally in response to some kind of computer emergency. As I learned from them, I soon realized that they were teaching me more than just nuts and bolts, and I began to seek out their counsel on issues ranging from the sociology of college students to church planting to the subcultures of the Millennial generation. Sometimes these R-mentors emerge from circumstances, and at other times we choose them. In the former case, a leader simply takes advantage of a precious, though unanticipated, opportunity, but in the latter she or he approaches the unlikely person(s) and begins learning by asking questions. Both scenarios require that the older leader exercise the power to choose, because the younger person is very unlikely to volunteer mentoring services.

Asking

The choice to define oneself as a protégé (although I have never heard a reverse mentor use this term) begins the process of conversation. Although these connections may be in person, by phone, or through a growing number of Internet channels, the principle remains the same: leadership development through simple dialogue. In longer-term P2P reverse mentoring, these talks often involve certain kinds of questions, albeit not necessarily in the order given here. The protégé must resist the temptation to offer answers to the answers. The process is not about talking; it's about asking questions:

- "How do I do this?" Asking for help with practical issues is the easiest way to begin a relationship with an R-mentor. Invariably, this kind of request produces a prompt outburst of helping behavior, parallel to the way your new friend helps her or his own parents in a similar predicament. Graciously accepting the help and thanking the younger person appropriately keeps the door open for more assistance in the future—a good thing, because you are going to need it. R-mentors, in turn, need to exhibit the same kind of graciousness, never making the protégé feel silly or disgraced by lack of skill.

- "Who or what is that?" A conversation sparked by technical assistance affords an opportunity to ask questions at the next level about the R-mentor's behaviors. If white wires dangle from their ears, the protégé might ask about the artist being listened to. When the R-mentor replies with the name of an obscure underground metal band from the Czech Republic, rather than backing off (and here's the key) press in by asking, "Who's that?" Even a small but authentic demonstration of interest in the other person's world opens the door to begin asking more detailed questions about something like their musical tastes. Things work best when the protégé avoids pressing too hard (as if interrogating a suspect or data-mining the Internet) and the mentor remains cooperative, even if the suspicion level rises a bit. If the mentor offers a response that seems intriguing but is unclear or too brief, the protégé can simply say, "Could you talk more about that?" If the R-mentor asks the reason for the questions, the mentee should be completely honest about wanting to learn from primary sources. Needless to say, pretending to be friends just to learn things corrupts the relationship into something ugly. Patronizing a protégé does the same.

• "Why is that?" Background information about the R-mentor's preferences supplies the raw material to begin inquiring about the much more important issue of *why* the younger person's world is arranged the way it is. Chances are the protégé will be the first person ever to ask this type of question. At this point, both parties benefit: the older leader gains valuable insight from a primary source while helping the younger mentor think through the reasons behind their default culture. Sometimes conversation stalls at this point because diagnosing the causes of social phenomena is difficult enough to occupy the whole field of sociology, and it may not be of any particular interest to the mentor just because the protégé asks. Patience at this juncture gives everyone a chance to consider the issue at length and often yields much more fruitful discussion in the future. In the interim, protégés must avoid the temptation to treat their newfound knowledge of three alternative rock bands as an insignia of youth or an excuse to drop their names at the next staff meeting as proof that they "get it," a tragic shift from asking back to talking.

• "Can you tell me a story?" Ethnographers studying subcultures place great value on the insights gained from narratives. In addition to other research tools, time spent listening to stories in common locations such as a local store can yield the kind of insight that makes sense out of quantitative studies.[6] Similarly, mentors often teach the most when they recount an event in their own lives, rather than just passing on things they observed or read. I have learned more about how young adults think by listening to them describe their daily lives than in any other way. One female staff pastor, for example, described the culture of her church's leadership by recounting a meeting in which she suggested that the ministry consider measuring its effectiveness by means other than just attendance. The deafening silence was followed by a group rebuke for the mere thought of using another standard. It hurt just to listen to her story, but it gave me a feel for how the young sometimes experience the practices of older leaders in a way that nothing else could have. Protégés need to remember that the stories are the most illuminating part of any meeting, not an alternative to *real* information. Mentors should interpret passages of the narrative beyond the understanding of their charges (what does it mean when I say a new DVD "dropped"?), and mentors must ask for a translation when one is not forthcoming.

• "What kind of relationship do we have?" At this point, the experience usually either proves a temporary help or shows signs of developing into something longer-term. The mentor and protégé will want to make the status of the relationship itself explicitly understood between them. This arrangement may mean the mentor agreeing to e-mail new cultural discoveries from time to time, a regular series of scheduled meetings, or simply the understanding that the protégé's office is always open for a drop-in visit. An open door tells the mentor that the relationship is valued more than the insights. The Harvard Business School's Monica Higgins points out in this regard: "Research suggests that a mentoring relationship works best when it evolves over time, in an informal fashion, through a shared interest in professional development. . . . Other research shows that effective mentoring relationships are those in which the communication styles of the mentor and the protégé match one another."[7] At this juncture, or perhaps earlier, all parties likely sense whether their styles match enough to proceed further or simply to harvest the benefits from the conversations so far and begin pursuing others. An RM association need not be long to offer the opportunity for important learning and real change.

The orderly questions presented here are actually a composite drawn from hundreds of conversations over several years. In real life, they almost never follow this pattern exactly because, outside of a mandatory R-mentoring system, these relationships simply refuse to obey a script—which is the best thing about them. This spontaneous quality, especially the wild unpredictability of what the protégé will learn, is a major source of the enjoyment and authenticity that keeps the friendship alive. Having dinner one night with Greg and a group of young friends, for example, we learned that among his peers marriage is considered to be only semiexclusive and semipermanent. Raised in the shadow of a divorce epidemic and saturated with media images of celebrity lifestyles, Greg's twentysomething friends enter marriage as an experiment in commitment and become involved with other partners fairly regularly because the experiment is only a general format for the relationship, not a binding covenant. In other words, everyone involved (especially the men, in Greg's view) retains free agent status. The point here is not the state of matrimony in the United States, but the ready availability of such powerful insights into the thinking of some young adult subcultures, insights that emerged spontaneously over Indian food. The greater our own commitment to the discipline of RM, the more these supposed accidents tend to happen.

Growing

If reverse mentoring on issues and problems leads to a more developed relationship, certain signature behaviors begin to appear:

- *Correction.* As a mentor and protégé build mutual respect, a point arrives at which the younger person feels enough trust in the relationship to offer outright correction to the older person. One of my R-mentors recently pointed out several flaws in some of my plans, while another punctured a cherished assumption about young adult ministry, and a third called me on misspelling the name of a popular band. Although those moments stung just a little, all of these friends meant well and all were sending a message something like "If our friendship is going to be for real, I have to be able to say this." Also, these mentors would have received the same from me. R-mentors should deliver these words very gently, and protégés should respond graciously.

- *Conflict.* With or without correction, R-mentoring relationships frequently involve some level of conflict between the parties owing to the obvious differences between them. Describing cross-cultural learning, urban specialists Conn and Ortiz advise "recognizing conflict as part of the learning experience . . . conflict often proves to be our friend, expanding our understanding in unexpected ways."[8] Without the ability to resolve difficult issues, like any other relationship our reverse mentoring partnerships will develop no further than the first disagreement.

- *Reciprocity.* A large proportion of my reverse mentoring experiences have developed over time into a mutual mentoring situation. The track record of the practice in the corporate world also offers many accounts of an older leader's strengths that ultimately help the younger mentor as much as or more than the reverse process. Typically, the R-mentor gains confidence and valuable insight from spending time with a senior leader; the latter picks up technical skills and greater cultural sensitivity. My role as protégé has led to a role as mentor in dozens of relationships. Developing mutuality in the association ultimately proves to be its most gratifying feature and stands as the test of maturity both for the participants and for their partnership.

One More Shot

The possibilities for reverse mentoring models are almost as diverse as the people available to participate in them. The hunger among leaders for something more than working harder within the limits of the same paradigm represents a rising tide among those I meet. One mid-fifties Christian educator described it this way: "I am convinced there are many of God's best seasoned leaders who don't know what to do at the season we are in, and are bored with leadership titles and roles in hierarchies of organizations, board meetings, but who now have the most value to add to younger generations, if they will do it out of friendship, not command-and-control types of leadership."

A learning relationship with the young offers a crucial element in revitalizing older leaders for "one more shot," and for development of the young who will continue on after our watch.

In a multiyear study of the three generations currently employed in the corporate sector, employee retention specialists Robin Throckmorton and Linda Gravett found that in practices such as reverse mentoring "the generations born furthest apart have the most to teach one another. . . . Once people start learning from each other, it combines the best elements of experience and innovation."[9] Embracing the diversity of RM models and accepting the reality of multiple, unanticipated outcomes, the process of asking questions and then listening—really listening—cultivates a powerful learning experience that ultimately benefits mentor and protégé alike.

11

PROCESSES

Embedding R-Mentoring in Organizations

Janet and I spotted the round, green Starbucks's logo on a billboard at exit 156, the middle of nowhere. Slowing for the exit ramp, we drove down an access road to a parking lot that hosted the coffee store. After ordering our usual drinks at the drive-through speaker, we pulled around to the pick-up window. I asked the young woman who handed me my cup for two of the short, bright green straws used when customers sample specialty beverages in miniature cups. Life on the road had taught me that folding the little straws in half made them the perfect size to jam into the hole in a coffee cup lid, preventing the expensive liquid inside from splashing out while driving a car. This simple trick had saved me many shirts and lots of coffee.

The staffer in the green apron admitted she had never heard of the straw trick, so she watched me demonstrate how to convert them into makeshift coffee lid stoppers. At the end of the brief lesson she said, "You taught me something today."

This member of the world's most influential coffee retailer lacked the knowledge that thousands, perhaps millions, of customers possessed: we love those little straws, and we want them *every time* we take our coffee out of the store. Despite years of market research, decades of experience, and a world-class training system, someone somewhere still thinks I just want coffee, when the truth is that I *want coffee that doesn't drip on my shirt.* If I have accomplished nothing else in the for-profit sector, at least I have the satisfaction of knowing that for a brief moment I worked as a reverse mentor for Starbucks.

This tiny incident speaks to the much larger challenge of developing R-mentoring procedures for organizations. My hands-on training session reached only one employee, whereas a whole company needs to know the magic of the straws. Fortunately, the kind of intercultural relationship with unlikely people that benefits an individual also holds potential for groups of people organized around a common purpose. Tom Kelley, head of the internationally known design firm Ideo, offers a simple example of what happens when insiders connect with outsiders: "If I just talk to my pals in their suburban homes, I might think everyone still watches TV. They don't. Now I know I'd better figure out a way to make a product live in cyberspace somewhere."[1] Responding to these perceived benefits, and catalyzed by the advent of the Internet, corporations began developing R-mentoring systems in the mid-1990s in hopes of capitalizing on the cultural and technological revolutions being led by the young.

The church is an exception. I find a handful of ministers with reverse mentors, a few denominational regions intentionally asking younger people to serve on their decision-making boards, and a couple of denominational "listening projects" generally set up as events in which young leaders are supposed to present their views to the organization's senior staff on a one-time basis. However, *I can cite no other examples of ministries with a coherent reverse mentoring process*. In one sense, this finding represents no surprise given the small size and single-staff format of most churches, the common reliance on volunteers, the unique dynamics of the nonprofit world, and the authoritarian tendencies of some ministry organizations. Ironically, all of these traits make borrowing strategies from huge corporations risky at best. Perhaps, though, as mentoring trainer Matt Starcevich concluded after a small online survey, some organizations simply practice the discipline without the label (the senior pastor asks the youth pastor to explain Emo music) or abandon the effort when lack of planning results in failure. He concludes, "The idea is good, but it needs help."[2] Providing this help through an intentional R-mentoring process suitable for the unique requirements of ministry leaders is the focus of this chapter.

Premise: A Culture, Not a System

Reverse mentoring initiatives in the for-profit sector, though not exactly parallel to the challenge of leading a ministry group, do offer a laboratory from which certain lessons emerge repeatedly enough to deserve our attention.

Diversity

The first and most obvious conclusion to be drawn from the for-profit and nonprofit sectors concerns the variety of available models. The RM marketplace bristles with unique approaches driven by the widely disparate contexts in which the practice is used and the creativity of those who use it. For example:

- A major book publisher places the operation of a marketing Website for teenagers in the hands of teens themselves.
- A global computer manufacturer keeps a teenager on staff in the office of the CEO.
- The U.S. Marine Corps begins requiring officers to submit their plans to the troops before they are carried out.
- A huge corporation converts an old warehouse, complete with a foosball table, into an "idea lab" staffed by hundreds of "e-belts" (black belts in e-business).
- A nonprofit organization deploys seventy-five thousand students from five hundred schools to help teachers integrate technology into classroom instruction.[3]

This sample only suggests the variety of experience available. I fell into the practice by accident and continued for quite a while before ever hearing the term *reverse mentoring*.

Perhaps this naiveté reflects the larger absence of the practice from ministry leadership circles, a void I experienced before stumbling into the benefits and the great fun of dialogue with the young. The lesson here for ministry leaders is that no matter what sort of approach they adopt to RM, they gain nothing by trying to copy someone else's model. There simply is no one superior approach to emulate. So the process of developing a process resembles an exploratory journey more than an experiment in cloning. Here are some ways to start.

Evolution

Descriptions of RM practices in any organization tend to be so brief and anecdotal (such as those just listed) that they generally constitute a snapshot that freezes the experience at one point in time. Although these examples offer helpful illustrations that suggest best practices, they are limited to presenting a "highlight reel" perspective that depicts the positives as if they all appeared on the first day of the program. With a decade of RM experience now available for examination (despite the continuing lack of a comprehensive quantitative study), a very different but unsurprising picture emerges: even huge institutions' approaches evolve over time. One example includes the supplanting of very formal, structured approaches typical of early R-mentoring initiatives in the 1990s with a much less formal, less long-term, less systematic philosophy in later years.[4] So highly scheduled relationships involving regular meetings and scripted agendas are giving way to "drop-in" RM in which the protégé takes advantage of a chance meeting to ask a question, or "on-demand" RM in which the protégé gets input from an R-mentor in response to a specific problem or issue. With the right relationships in place, the structures of the early days tend to become less necessary. The Wharton School's Jerry Wind offers a second illustration: "In today's environment, more executives and CEOs are comfortable with technology. . . . Now, it's more of the students providing them with a different perspective on the younger generation. Reverse mentoring is a very powerful concept if you broaden it beyond just the narrow technical area."[5] Responding to the rapid integration of portable computing with Internet connectivity in the hands of those under thirty, early renditions of RM tended to operate within a technological silo defined by the needs of older leaders, suggesting a starting point obvious for the time, like teaching the boss how to use e-mail or operate a PDA. Ten years later, that boss is enjoying retirement while the new boss, familiar with e-mail and a Blackberry expert, carries on oblivious to social networking sites and the global power of hip hop.

Second-generation RM, then, while continuing to involve tech training, leans much more toward cultural insight, market understanding, and stimulating creativity with young thinking in organizations dominated by old ways. The point becomes new relationships, not just a new way of catching up on our technological skill set. For ministry leaders, the implication here is that regardless of how an RM process begins, evolution over time seems to be a normal part of the experience rather than a sign that the original concept failed. In fact, embracing these changes is the best way to keep the process alive and well in your ministry. If you think of yourself as somewhere on an RM scale of 1 to 10, with 1 being no experience at all and 10 representing a very regular discipline, you have the first clue about how to get going. The closer you are to the 10 end of the scale, the more ready you are to think in terms of putting together a system for your ministry. Those nearer the 1 end should begin with simple personal experiences to get the feel for how the whole relationship works, because a system is simply that relationship writ large.

Planning

Virtually every commentator on the history and development of RM systems recommends the implementation cycle typical for any new program: form consensus, create plans, train participants, evaluate results, etc. In fact, Starcevich states bluntly that his online survey indicates "there is nothing unique about reverse mentoring. These same challenges need to be managed in any mentoring relationship. The operative word is mentoring."[6] His argument is that virtually nothing unique or special is necessary to develop an RM system. Following this logic, anyone capable of operating an effective conventional mentoring process can expect the same level of success running an RM system. Except for one thing: it's all in reverse.

Traditional mentoring seldom gives rise to fear or embarrassment for the older partner; nor does it tempt the young to exhibit a condescending or intimidating attitude. Flattening the hierarchy that separates two people is the primary contributor to the effectiveness of R-mentoring because it closes the power distance between them, minimizing the fear of consequences that comes with it. However, the conventional approach, with its many benefits, operates by capitalizing on hierarchy (the senior position or greater experience of the mentor) for the benefit of the protégé. Both offer substantial benefits, but vastly less research and precedent are available on the reverse variety. So it would seem reasonable that an RM system is not simply a conventional mentoring system upside down.

However, perhaps the one thing we do know conclusively is that failing to plan an RM process effectively creates conditions that almost guarantee failure, possibly inoculating the ministry against the prospect of ever trying again. Much later, this kind of failure may echo in the phrase "We tried that once before." Starting up a ministry-based RM process, then, involves much more than a sermon on the subject citing biblical illustrations (like the servant girl described in 2 Kings whose advice led to the healing of Namaan's leprosy) or a staff meeting spent reviewing the track record of Jack Welch at GE. The fruitfulness of RM will rise and fall on the quality of the plan used to implement and guide it.

If anything, ministry leaders start too many programs. The process is no mystery. But sending memos, requiring meetings, and demanding progress reports generally secures procedural conformity without much real change on an individual or organizational level. Going along becomes a counterfeit for growing effectiveness. Developing an effective RM plan, then, means thinking of it not as the blueprint of a *system* but as the catalyst for a *culture*.

Promise: A Ministry to Our Ministry

Forming a culture is much more difficult but much more rewarding than just requiring a new activity. I witnessed the distinction firsthand during my days as a seminary professor. Deeply concerned about improving the quality of student writing and the quantity of faculty writing, our new dean, Joe Castleberry, made the shocking announcement during a faculty meeting that, after reviewing all of the solutions employed by major institutions, he regretted to announce that none of them worked. Writing clinics, personal tutoring, self-help programs, and many other options had all been tried everywhere from Harvard to the local junior college with some positive results, but without success consistent enough to make them reliable. In short, nothing worked. Joe then presented the idea of keeping some backstops in place to help students (such as "writing probation" for those really struggling) but concentrating much more on creating what he called a "culture of writing," led from the front by a faculty that published more regularly and reinforced by celebrating and rewarding publication as a tangible objective of the seminary. Values began to accomplish what structures alone could not. The plan for the new culture included just enough specific steps to form a pathway for the advancement of the values it represented. Quantifying the aggregate results is difficult, but there is little doubt that everyone benefited. In fact, it was in this culture that my first book was written and this book developed.

Converting the individual practice of reverse mentoring into a collective spiritual discipline, then, means thinking of it as a new culture, as a ministry to our ministry, one requiring the assets that all spiritual leaders have depended on before.

Exemplary Leaders

Reverse mentoring in the corporate world doubtless owes much of its early popularity to Jack Welch. Though not the first to try the procedure, he was likely the first well-known CEO to use it *personally*, tapping thirtysomething Pam Wickham from GE's public relations staff to teach him the basics of the Internet one-on-one.[7] Hundreds of other executives within the company began R-mentoring relationships by fiat, but Welch went first, developing a partnership with Wickham by choice rather than mandate.

This often overlooked aspect of what would become the most-cited example of RM in the for-profit world bears emphasizing with ministry leaders. In our search for organizational solutions to our problems, we sometimes forget that our influence comes not from "lording it over those entrusted to you but being examples to the flock."[8] Christian leaders who make the first move, taking the risk of setting a personal precedent, will discover that this individual decision sways their group in ways no systemic component can match. In fact, the absence of personal involvement by leadership probably spells doom for any RM process eventually, no matter how refined the method appears at the outset. In one of the listening projects with which I am familiar, for example, a significant opportunity to catalyze R-mentoring throughout a denomination was lost when senior leadership proved startlingly unable to hear the views of the young without describing them as "disrespectful." Word of this attitude spread through the ranks of young leaders like an urban legend and rendered much of this national initiative fruitless.

Credible Urgency

Leaders willing to set the example and then help their ministry consider the value of reverse mentoring can use specific examples to help those within the ministry come to terms with both the need for RM and the simple ways in which it can be incorporated into the group's life. These examples can start with recognizing ministry deficits as small as a lack of video editing skill and as large as the failure to appeal to outsiders. Or illustrations can be drawn from the vital assets our unlikely friends offer, such as a native understanding of youth culture. Case studies from other organizations can also help, especially if a representative is available to speak to your group. The more this urgency is defined as a pursuit of advantages rather than a solution to problems, the greater the ministry's likely receptivity. A simple exercise like asking a twenty-year-old to visit with your senior staff for an hour, or showing your team several YouTube videos, can jolt them into realizing that their grip on the issues of the day may not be as tight as they think. I have witnessed this effect firsthand in the earlier part of this century when LaDonna Witmer's video "This Is Who I Am" electrified older audiences with a first-hand account of Gen X culture delivered as a performance piece. After viewing it, older leaders started scrambling to learn more, responding to the power of a primary source.

Reasonable Expectations

Even if modeled by leadership and couched in compelling terms, RM may meet with jadedness about yet "another new program," which is how it will be seen until it becomes a culture. The best antidote for this attitude is the kind of realism that describes everything about RM, including its risk factors (such as patronizing mentors) and its time penalties. This realism requires not inflating the immediate payoffs and not insisting that everyone embrace the idea at first exposure. It also means explaining that the process always changes over time and that outright failure is a live option.

With assumptions of this kind in place, leadership is in a position to propose an experiment aimed at testing the potential of RM as a new form of ministry to our ministry. One handy kind of experimentation involves asking a few willing staff members or volunteers to try a short-term (perhaps thirty-day), single issue (say, outsider attitudes toward worship services) one-on-one R-mentoring experiment and then debrief their experience with the larger group. The debrief session models the process that leadership can use later to monitor the progress of reverse mentoring in their ranks. The (usually very positive) results will help build both a shared urgency and a commonsense view of how the process might work in the real world of their ministry. Jim Henderson's book *Jim & Casper Go to Church*,[9] for instance, chronicles the travels of Henderson and his atheist friend Matt Casper through a number of churches, some of which are quite high-profile. The results are so eye-opening to church insiders that Jim and Matt now speak together (and separately) at Christian conferences and churches, which is where I met them both. This simple excursion into RM could easily be duplicated in any local venue where leaders were willing to invite even one outsider friend to a Sunday morning service for the express purpose of receiving a "review." Explaining that the first rendition of R-mentoring need not last longer than a few weeks or months, and that the practice serves well in either an ongoing or a case-by-case mode, suggests an appealing lack of rigidity in the culture. The open architecture of the planning process, then, creates a climate that fosters the kind of experimentation that can help to customize RM models from the fairly generic form in which they started.

Healthy Relationships

Reverse mentors are friends, not magicians. They "won't tell you exactly what to do or how to do it," says 3M executive and reverse mentoring veteran Robin Torgerson, "but they'll help you figure that out for yourself. It helps make you a better, smarter person."[10] That is, if you are already a pretty good person. Leaders who could mandate RM relationships across the board should resist the temptation to apply the practice like fluoride in public drinking water. In reality, reverse mentoring works best when it capitalizes on healthy associations exhibiting traits such as good communication, deference, trust, and personal compatibility.[11] Attempting to learn from R-mentoring while simultaneously expecting it to rehabilitate dysfunctional people or groups serves no one well in the end. One mentoring research project, for example, including a massive ten-year literature review and a large-scale statistical study of employee attitudes, found that the quality of the mentoring *relationship* shaped the attitude of employees toward their work and career more than anything else, including the method of matching mentors with protégés and the amount of structure and formality in the program.[12] Some of the keys to health in these relationships:

• *Choice.* Common sense and field research both recommend that protégés who choose their mentors generally enjoy a more positive experience, perhaps because they intuitively seek out healthier relationships.[13]

• *Purpose.* Mentors and protégés who negotiate the exact reason for their partnership experience fewer misunderstandings and eliminate a major reason RM relationships sometimes fail.

• *Unlikeliness.* Drawing mentors from outside the organization or the department offers the best chance for long-term success because it minimizes complications.

• *Training.* Simple instructions from leadership should include issues such as sticking to a schedule of meetings, keeping written notes, maintaining reasonable confidentiality, and expecting to debrief in some form that benefits the overall ministry. One study finds, in fact, that training mentors raises the success rate by 65 percent, while training both mentors and protégés raises it by almost 90 percent.[14] With so much at stake, leadership needs to invest in both initial and ongoing training for all of its protégés and as many of its mentors as are available.

- *Debriefing.* Processing the raw data from R-mentoring encounters in small groups seems to be an especially effective way to integrate these insights into the future of the ministry.

- *Patterns.* Mentor-protégé partnerships involve a learning curve that seems quite steep at first. The struggle revolves less around the subject discussed than the relationship that makes the discussion possible. Drawing from his own experience with two reverse mentors, Tom Kelley comments on the awkwardness of the first talk: "That's the reason it's such a good idea," he says, "having the first conversation means it never has to be awkward again." In Kelley's case, he learned how to set up a blog for an online magazine from one R-mentor, and he found out why young adults have abandoned wristwatches.[15] Although informality in the planning and culture of an R-mentoring process is commendable, the actual relationships generally benefit from a bigger dose of structure most commonly found in a schedule for meeting that is agreed on in advance and then adhered to, including time limits. An agreement between mentors and protégés to meet at least twice, for example, gives them the opportunity to push through the awkward phase and build enough trust to begin learning.

Open Channels

Thinking of reverse mentoring only as two nervous people sitting in an office or coffeehouse exchanging questions and answers greatly limits its potential. Widening the options for meeting venues, subjects, and modes of contact can make the potential benefits more accessible.

- *Variety.* An entire leadership team may invest in R-mentoring on a single issue (for instance, Web 2.0) or divide up a variety of topics, about which to approach an eclectic set of mentors who may not necessarily be young.

- *Excursions.* Some of the best reverse mentoring happens through immersion in an alien environment, as when Ford engineers and marketers visited a London hair salon in an attempt to understand the young people who were about to become their next generation of customers. The connection with these brand-conscious young people changed them from marketing demographics into actual people with actual preferences. The insights gained by the Ford staff proved so profound that they began developing automotive designs for review by the young adults they met in the excursion, asking them, "Would you want a vehicle like this?" The result is a radically consumer-driven design process that is being imported to the United States by the same company, meaning that thousands of Ford employees will be making similar trips to grocery stores and dance clubs to meet young consumers up close and learn from them.[16] Protégés encouraged to get out of the office for field trips when their R-mentor is available to serve as a cultural interpreter reap the greatest reward from the practice. Hearing about body art is one thing; hearing about it while standing in the tattoo parlor where your mentor got his is something else. Using common-sense standards of appropriateness for these site visits will keep you informed without getting into trouble.

- *Modes.* Protégés need not confine their mentoring sessions to the face-to-face format. Increasingly, for-profit enterprises turn to Internet-based models sometimes referred to as "global mentoring," in which employees seek out counsel from thousands of others working for their firm around the world.[17] All types of mentoring (traditional, group, peer) flow through these systems in a torrent of online relationships, with explosive growth implying that this mode represents a very important aspect of the future of reverse mentoring. As one beneficiary of this model notes, "If I am considering moving to Hong Kong, I can find a mentor in Hong Kong. If I'm doing business in Russia, I can find someone."[18] Perhaps the most interesting way to launch RM as a ministry to our ministry, then, could involve using Web-savvy outside mentors to help design a twenty-first-century approach in which they could communicate with protégés via e-mail, blogs, instant messaging, and so on. Because technological issues often serve as the on ramp to other subjects, this exercise itself might ignite the reverse mentoring discipline in the ministry. The pharmaceutical firm Abbot found, for example, that introduction of an online mentoring system led to such rapid expansion that in only two years the system hosted 930 mentors and more than 1,600 protégés. A management consulting firm testing the idea of online mentoring hoped to recruit 500 participants but received applications from that many mentors, ending up with 750 participants, 95 percent of whom are in active mentoring relationships. As the Internet expands its presence in all aspects of our lives and ministries, it is only natural that we should consider online modes as a legitimate way of doing mentoring of all kinds, including the reverse variety.[19]

Customizing an RM process involves combining these elements in a way, and at a time, that shapes the practice to the culture of a ministry organization. Consider the possible combinations as represented in general terms in the diagram shown here.

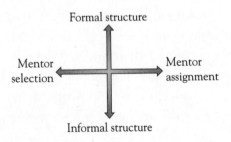

Formal structure

Mentor selection ← → Mentor assignment

Informal structure

Groups comfortable with a formal style can highlight structure, schedule, and assigned partners, while more free-wheeling shops can emphasize voluntary associations, experimentation, and the power of the accidental. This sort of flexibility is common in the corporate world, where one marketing firm will rely almost exclusively on surveys, structured, interviews, and the kind of observation I experienced the evening I was part of a test audience for several new sitcoms (which never saw the light of day). The researchers asked us to watch segments of each program and then take paper-and-pencil tests that asked us which kinds of products were brought to mind when we saw the shows. Somewhere, someone believed this approach was science. Other friends in the marketing business, who are just as capable, do their research by choosing venues likely to attract influential personalities (say, the local coffeehouse) and simply meet people with the intention of asking them questions about issues related to the products the firm is going to promote. Both sides would make a case for their approach, but ministry leaders need to have all these options open so that their RM system is a good fit for their setting. The critical issue is that everyone involved finds the hands-on reverse mentoring experience to be fruitful and fun. Without both outcomes, the discipline slips into a dull habit and eventually dies. But when developed as a culture and a set of relationships rather than a system, reverse mentoring spreads spontaneously beyond what any process requires. As a ministry to our ministry, it encourages leadership development by cultivating the humility that gives the discipline life. What might happen if a church actually took this idea seriously?

Big Box Church

The staff at Big Box Church sensed something was wrong. Even though their attendance remained the envy of other congregations, and their financial bottom line looked good, some gloomy clouds darkened the horizon. First-time visitors still regularly found their church largely because it was just off the beltway, but follow-up phone calls and visits revealed them to be mainly believers, some new to the community and others considering a transfer to Big Box to join the growing ranks of the "rechurched" worshipping there on Sunday morning.

The missional focus so close to the church's heart when it was founded less than ten years before seemed to be growing fuzzier by the year as the number of baptisms declined imperceptibly and reports of God's deeds in their midst crept away from the dramatic stories of the pioneer days. Commercial videos purchased by the staff to illustrate sermons seemed more powerful than firsthand accounts of what God was doing. Exactly what *was* God doing anyway?

The influence of well-intentioned long-term members was also shifting away from bringing unchurched visitors and toward a swelling concern with the facility and finances, and something they called "family ministry." Unknown to the staff, these members shared the same gnawing sense that, even though things were not bad, neither were they what they had been when Big Box was only a small box in town.

During one of those intrusions of grace that make an ordinary meeting memorable for a lifetime, Ed, the senior pastor, surfaced this simmering concern in front of both staff and key lay leaders, all of whom realized to their great relief that they were essentially on the same page but had simply never looked at that page together. Although local ministers viewed Big Box as a thriving success story, the core leadership sensed the fragility of their condition, realizing that in a few more years on their current trajectory whatever was wrong now could turn them into a sad parody of what the group had started out to be. Their attendance might continue to grow, but their sense of mission to the community might be a casualty in the process.

Ed stepped into a moment of silence in the conversation and admitted that his sensitivity to Big Box's predicament had developed in a strange way. When he stopped one day for a cappuccino at his favorite coffee shop, he started talking to one of their employees, a young man half his age. This encounter led to an ongoing series of lengthening, freewheeling conversations about life, culture, and spirituality. Brent described himself as very spiritual but with a strong distaste for what he called "organized religion," to which he attributed many of the planet's ills. His spiritual journey included some childhood exposure to Christian worship services, but since then he seemed to have sampled everything else in varying combinations. Ed thought of him as "Buddhist lite" but never said that out loud.

In their regular chats, he and Brent discussed many aspects of their lives, but they seemed to return to spiritual things more often than not. Brent had never known a minister before and liked having one as a friend, but Ed was troubled by the fact that he couldn't really remember the last time he had spent regular time with an outsider. So many meetings. . . .

Their conversations became more difficult when they turned to the subject of the church, with Brent insisting that he wanted nothing to do with judgmental Christians wasting money on huge buildings as the world starved. Doing his best to explain, Ed realized that for now the way to love Brent was to show him the respect of continuing to ask questions. He never won a debate because he never turned their friendship into one, but he did catch just a glimpse of Brent's perspective on places like Big Box. Doing so made him realize, he told the leadership, that when looking out over the Sunday morning crowd faces like Brent's just were not there.

Ed then asked if everyone in the room would be willing to consider finding a Brent of their own from whom to learn. Big Box had a mission statement and set of values so persuasive that other churches copied it regularly, but some intangible element of their life together seemed to be slipping away. Everyone said all the right things, but their impact on the community was clearly changing, and not for the better. The congregation had more funds to invest in programming and service than ever before, but the leadership sensed they were sending dollars where they used to send people.

After some questions about how a plan like this might work, the staff and lay leadership agreed to identify outsiders willing to talk with them at least four times in the next two months. Some would form neighborhood groups, others would meet with a friend for coffee every other week, and still others would try to have individual talks with four people. Along the way, some of the conversations never happened and others went badly, but enough of them took place (even though they were uncomfortable) for these leaders to collect raw data. Some of the relationships continued beyond the initial phase to become enjoyable friendships.

Two months later, Ed asked the leadership team to meet again to debrief their experience. "So, what did we learn?" he asked. One leader looked up and said quietly, "We don't get Brent. And until we do, he's not going to get us."

Unlikely Conversations

Listening to the unlikely allows leaders to hear things available in no other way. As Tom Peters puts it, "If your top management isn't spending at least a half an hour, say, a month sitting down with someone twenty five years old or younger, then they are blowing it."[20] This could be said for any younger person who isn't doing the same with the old. A similar principle applies to insiders and outsiders, speakers and audiences, and leaders and followers. Reverse mentoring systems offer the opportunity for many more of these unlikely conversations to happen, not because they have to happen but because we want them to.

12

INTERVIEW

Joel and Rachel Mentor Earl and Janet

Accounts of reverse mentoring in the corporate and nonprofit sectors feature certain common traits. One involves evaluating the benefits and pitfalls of the process almost exclusively from the standpoint of the protégé. Jack Welch's experience at General Electric represents the paradigm case, with him and other executives like him cited and quoted in many accounts almost to the exclusion of the reverse mentors themselves. Though some reports offer an exception, the basic rule for writing on this subject seems to be reliance on the opinions of the most powerful people involved. Perhaps this trait in the literature has to do with the shock value involved when an older person in a corner office becomes the student of a younger person who doesn't even have an office. In the business world especially, that's news.

This chapter lets reverse mentors reflect on the experience in their own words, something they seldom get to do. In October 2006, the Assemblies of God Theological Seminary (AGTS) hosted a one-day conference around my book *Off-Road Disciplines: Spiritual Adventures of Missional Leaders*.[1] One segment of the event focused on the subject of reverse mentoring and featured an interview with Joel and Rachel Triska, both in their twenties, students at AGTS and our mentors. My wife, Janet, and I interviewed the Triskas, whom we had known for about two years, in front of the seminar audience of around 150 ministers and seminary staff. The questions were informal and the interview took place without formal preparation. No one knew what was going to happen. In keeping with this approach, the transcript appears here with only very minor editing for the purpose of clarity.

My friend Dwight, who pastors a large church in the Midwest, once told me that my "functional age" seemed younger to him than my chronological age. One survey reports that Baby Boomers feel an average of eleven years younger than the calendar indicates, but I think Dwight detected something more, an influence on my behavior by younger people such as Joel and Rachel with whom we spend time.[2] It was from them that I first learned about blogging as a new form of communication and then launched my own primitive Xanga, which led to MySpace, which led to Facebook, which will almost certainly lead to an exploration of virtual reality. I also learned about Internet video telephony using Skype, how to replace a goatee with a soul patch, and the raw power of video parodies (especially when serving as the object). But beyond technical skills and cultural perspective, we have found Joel and Rachel to be wonderful friends. They give us hope for the next generation of Christian leaders.

When asked by someone in the seminar audience how I kept up with cultural trends, I pointed at the Triskas and said:

> I might have coffee with Joel and Rachel, we'll maybe just bump into each other and I'll say, "Did you see X on the Internet yesterday?" and they'll say, "Yeah, we've been watching that for a year." And I'll say, "Is that popular, is that a thing?" And so these guys are my first filter, they help me to know what needs to be paid attention to and what doesn't and, oh man, is that a huge thing. Because that makes 99 percent of everything else fall away and you can focus on the 1 percent. It's not about being young, it's about being tuned in.

Our relationship represents an example of the generations working together. It is one that could be replicated frequently if everyone were willing. The more we hear from reverse mentors in their own words, the easier it is to become willing.

Interview

Earl: Maybe we could just begin by saying how we actually
  met, which was kind of an "off-road" adventure of its own.

Joel: Rachel and I call this my "postmodern crisis."

Rachel: I prayed for someone to come and save him.

Joel: I read a book, and books can tend to mess you up a bit,
  but this was called *Stories of Emergence*,[3] and all these
  emerging people were writing stories. I was a youth pastor for about three years and this was about two years into
  that, and I began to read this book, and it began to bring
  forward some questions in me that I had been pushing
  back, and they began coming to the forefront, and I didn't
  know how to deal with them. So in this book was a chapter
  written by Earl, and I was reading where you were from,
  and I saw "A/G" connected to it and I said, "Oh, I'm going
  to e-mail this guy." I had never done anything like that
  before and I just sent this e-mail that brought up this, "Hey
  you don't know me but, like, help me."

  The next day I got this e-mail back and he signed it
  "E," not "Dr. Earl Creps." That spoke volumes to me, like,
  how he thought of himself. And before you know it, Earl
  and Janet and Rachel and myself were sitting at Panera
  Bread and just kind of hanging out. That's what just kind
  of led to our decision to come here to AGTS.

Earl: How do you guys see what happened from there?

Rachel: It was a cool experience. I guess it was February 2004
  when we first met and Joel and I went back and forth—was
  AGTS the right thing for us, and we were like, "Well,
  Earl's there, so we'll go." You know, we'll go because Earl's
  there, and if nothing else we will get to know Earl and
  Jan better, and we just really connected with you guys.
  So we came and knew he doesn't really teach that many
  master-level courses, so how are we going to get in to get
  to know this couple because we really think they have a
  lot to teach us. So we started scheming and conniving and

Joel was like, "We are just going to start calling them and visiting them," and it was really cool 'cause in our minds we thought "We are going to have to work really hard to make this happen."

But once we took the first step Jan and Earl just kind of enveloped us and started bringing us along on their journey of life. And it was one of the coolest experiences for us because they brought us into their home, they've taken us with them on trips, and in that process Earl described what happens whenever you have mentoring and reverse mentoring going on at the same time: it's a beautiful marriage, and that's really what we have experienced with our friendship with them. It's one of the healthiest mentoring relationships I think we have ever had, just in the sense that it's really a give-and-take and not just a give, give, give or take, take, take. It's really been a great experience.

Joel: I was schooled in the John Maxwell approach, where you bring a hundred dollars and pay someone for their hour and learn whatever they know best and tuck that away in your files, and then you never see each other again. So the idea that we can have something to bring to the table was incredibly validating. It was good to see that my perspective had a valid point too.

Janet: In the youth ministry that you guys were in, what do you see as your most single topic or challenge that you would have liked to talk with older leaders about at that time—a challenge in your ministry that you would have liked to have had dialogue about?

Joel: Oh, man, I think for us we started understanding what those differences were and being able to talk about them. A lot of things Rachel and I talk about, it's not that we think we understand them better, or deserve to have the power (we don't have the experience for that), but we do have a perspective that we would like to be heard sometimes. We feel like we have brains, we are at least

semi-intelligent people; we see the same world everyone
else sees, we can make some observations that have some
validity. Couldn't we talk about those too? And so that's
one of the main things that we just really wanted—when
we have leaders we *want* them to lead us, we *want* them
to challenge us, and we want them to push us, but we
also want them to feel like they understand us, too. And
nothing is worse than being led by someone that doesn't
understand you.

Earl: You know, on that subject, I would probably have a
bunch of answers to this in my head, but from the time we
have spent together, how do *you* understand us as being
different? I mean as two couples, from two different generations, when you talk to your friends about us, about how
weird we are and about how hopeless we are. How do you
see us?

Janet: Don't be too specific please. . . .

Joel: OK, first of all, you guys are a phenomenon—so we kind
of have to lay the ground rules. You are a bit of an exception to the rule. But generally, obviously technology is
huge, but I think the first perspective we see beyond that is
this whole morphing postmodern perspective. For me personally, I just felt that I was really indoctrinated with the
idea that you have to be so confident, almost cocky with
your perspective; that's the way you carry it. For a while
I learned that, and I lived that, and it just didn't gel with
the world that I was growing up in—my peers, the culture I
was raised in—and I had to unlearn all that. And so I think
that probably in all that Rachel and I had to go through
the major dividing point is that you have to understand
something that you weren't raised up in. And I know that's
really a generalization, but I think that's probably what
most people my age would say.

Rachel: A lot of things are different; it's not a character difference, it's more something inherent and living in a

generation going through that, you know these things. So whenever you are sitting down with an adult and you are explaining something to them and they are just not getting it and you're going, "It's so obvious," but you can't say that because there's like this wall and you can't go through this wall and say what you mean: "OK, man, you just don't get it here!" It's a very rare relationship you can have with an adult, which is one of the rare and unique things about our relationship with Earl and Janet; they have given us the freedom that, whenever they just aren't getting something, we can actually say, "You guys just don't get this one."

If I could ask for other adults to give one freedom to younger people that they really respect and value, it would be the freedom to sometimes be able to say, "You don't get it." And even if you don't agree with them, just let them explain *why* they think you don't get it. Because there is a reason. It's not because we've come to the table wanting to be critical of people who are older. One of the comments I made to Earl recently during one of our conversations is that being in this relationship with them is probably one of the most humbling experiences of my life; because for someone that you respect and who is older and wiser and has lived life and has done so much more than you and you want to emulate to come to you and say, "Teach me." You go, "Who am I?" And the fact is that Earl and Janet really believe that Joel and I have something to offer them; that it's not just a gesture, but they believe that we have something that we can bring to the table that can make life and ministry some-how better. And that's a whole lot more humbling to me than something that would increase pride or arrogance; it puts me in my place quicker than anything else.

Earl: Are there things that you would like to be able to say to older leaders in general on this subject that might make it easier for them to take hold of it and seem like something they would like to be a part of?

Joel: I think that primarily the first rock that would have to
be taken out of someone's hand, is the idea that this is
all about a difference in style—it's not. For me, it feels so
much bigger. Whether it's European jeans or whatever the
new style that's coming through, for us it's much bigger.
It's a mind-set, it's a worldview, it's a way of approaching
things. I think for leaders that kind of balk at giving space
for criticism, you are going to have people who are going
to have their criticisms; you have arrogant people everywhere. But for the most part, at least Rachel and our peers
are usually pretty aware of the contributions that Builders
and Boomer generations before have made and aren't going
to overstep; we respect boundaries.

And most younger leaders are going to take great
honor in being asked what they think. The way Rachel
and I do with you. We take great honor in that you care
what we think. And we would never abuse that. I mean we
protect that. We would never want you to have reason to
take that away. And most people our age feel that way, and
given the opportunity to share, to contribute to someone's
life whom we naturally feel is wiser and more experienced.
I mean "encouraging" is way too light a word to use.

Earl: Well, you guys know us pretty well. You've had tenure
in what we call the "faculty of our life" for a while now, so
speak to us as faculty. Where do we need to go from here?
We've talked about a lot of different things, technology,
culture, fashion, music, postmodernism, etc. If we could
be asking about certain things now, what would you hope
those issues would be?

Joel: One thing, and I think we find this across the board, is
that we place great value in finding unity within diversity.
And we realize that within your generation most of the
power is there, and to create that kind of change we would
ask you to really look at that issue and help us make that
happen. Bring some unity in our diversity.

Janet: My approach is a little more simple and a little more maternal. My heart is just to offer young adults a place at the table, a place where they feel they belong, where they feel they are a part of us—instead of "These people over here, they are our sons, our daughters." And if they can feel they are important and they are significant and moreover they have potential in God and they are encouraged and have purpose in life. All this other stuff is important, but that's the main focus, just that they would have a place at the table. And that when we leave we can leave a legacy of them knowing they are important and knowing that they belong.

Rachel: Honestly, this is something that Joel and I have already talked about, and in our lives of knowing Earl and Jan and what they have contributed to our lives and bringing us along on the journey with them. A couple of weeks ago, they spoke in Kansas City and they took us with them and set us in a situation like this where we were able to share, and they do things like that on a regular basis of bringing us along with them and letting us see how they live life and how they do ministry and how they do marriage, and it's just such a practical way of mentoring. And Joel and I have had this conversation, "We will do this. This isn't just something that we are going to take in and be a beneficiary of, but this is something that we will practice in our life and it's a choice and it's a decision that we have made." And even this last week, the four of us were having a conversation about MySpace and I said, "I don't know the answer to that question."

But I work at Evangel University with students from eighteen to twenty-four, and I can certainly find out the answer. So I went back to my dorm and I e-mailed the girls and I said, "Look I'm not old, but I'm not culture-savvy enough to know the answer to this question, can you help me out?" And I had twenty-seven different girls e-mail me responses and talk to me, and so even now it's something we are beginning to practice and realize that I was one of those students who was sitting in the class saying "I've passed cool . . . I'm no longer at the peak of cool anymore." And now working with these college students, who are really not very much younger than me but know so much more than I do, especially in culture, I realize that they are my teachers in a lot of ways, and if I want to be effective on the college campus I can't think that I know everything, but I have to go to the students and say, "I don't understand this, can you help me?" And I don't know if I would have been as open to that even now if Earl and Janet hadn't modeled it for us.

You Can't Rebel Against Helplessness

I never knew being a protégé could be so much fun. Our relationship with Joel and Rachel demonstrates that, in the words of the Harvard Business School's Rosabeth Moss Kanter, R-mentoring doesn't "wipe out the traditional kind . . . the best mentoring works in both directions."[4] This premise finds validation over and over in our relationship, a partnership in which we are all students. Perhaps more than anything else, their gracious attitude helps to desensitize us to the pain of saying "I don't get it." In fact, in several years of serving as a protégé, I have yet to encounter hostility or condescension. Thus the great strength of framing reverse mentoring as a friendship rather than a one-shot best practice stems from the kind of vulnerability required to develop a real relationship. For example, journalist Cindy Krischer Goodman, discussing the response of experienced reporters to R-mentoring, notes that "I received lots of feedback from colleagues who want me to know they no longer feel any shame in tapping into the expertise of those who are younger."[5] Respectful friendships foster dropping our guard until admission of need becomes a path to mutual learning. As one market researcher put it, "You can't rebel against helplessness."[6]

At the conclusion of the interview, we opened the floor for questions from the assembled ministers. One of the first people to take the microphone asked, "I think it's great that you are looking to them to find what they have to offer. What is it that you have to offer them? What is it you hope they get from you?" My answer dealt with the fact that one of our mentors will someday have a conversation with someone who is a third their age and it will go something like, "Weren't you guys around back when people used the Internet?" At that moment, they will be us and will have a choice to make. More than anything else, an older protégé hopes to leave an example that will help someone who is young today do the same thing when that season of life arrives. The frenzy of change in which we live renders information and experience obsolete at a frightening pace, while making personal character and spiritual depth more valuable than ever. With their peers, then, our mentors will face the challenge of saying, "I don't get it—can you teach me?" I believe they are up to it.

Epilogue

I WAS SO MUCH OLDER THEN; I'M YOUNGER THAN THAT NOW

My journey into the unconventional practice of reverse mentoring began in an unconventional way, years before I ever heard the term. In the summer of 2001 I found myself marooned in the Los Angeles area, having discovered too late that a couple of doctoral courses I hoped to take had been rescheduled. With the travel commitment already made, Byron Klaus, the president of AGTS, encouraged me to make the trip anyway as a way of doing field research on a cluster of young leaders just starting to carry the tag "emerging church." Early signs indicated something important was developing, and this sojourn on the coast offered an opportunity to find out what these new ways of thinking looked like in practice. I headed to California to spend time in a class taught by a famous person, only to discover another classroom on the street.

My first stop was Spencer Burke's house. With the help of friends, he developed theOOZE.com into one of the first and definitely most influential Websites concerned with emerging culture. Word on the street was that theOOZE also served as the *New York Times* of younger leaders. When I e-mailed, Spencer invited me to meet him and coworker Matt Palmer in their "international corporate headquarters"—the garage attached to the back of his house. As a seminary professor from the Midwest dropping into this beach town Internet nexus, I felt just a little out of place. Spencer and Matt did their best to make me feel at home as I set up my tripod and video camera to shoot a Hi-8mm video of an interview with them. Hustling to put my borrowed equipment together, they gave me a background briefing on why their site started and how its global reach was managed from a couple of computers sitting on a long table in a small garage. With everything just about ready, I prepared to turn the camera on and launch into a list of questions about postmodernism (then the topic du jour). As I reached for the Record button, Spencer said gently, "You know, this all might go better if you take the lens cap off."

That simple statement captured a guiding metaphor. Reverse mentoring is the process of taking off our lens covers, of removing the obstacles to unlikely relationships and the transformational learning that they involve. Removing the lens cap with great embarrassment led to an interview, which led to a cheeseburger, which led to a friendship that I enjoy and benefit from to this day. The "unlikeliness" in this bond is primarily things such as culture (blue state versus red state) and ministry context (Web versus seminary). I spent years in universities to become a teacher only to find myself learning more in two hours from Spencer and Matt than some professors taught me in months. But the most important thing discovered that day in the garage was the power of an unobstructed lens.

R-mentoring, then, helps us develop skills through knowledge transfer and experience transformation through clarifying vision in ways that reconnect our ministries with culture. I have found the former influence often leading to the latter in three basic forms:

1. *R-mentoring breaks me.* The first time I go to a much younger person and say the four dreaded words, "I am not cool," or "I don't get it," something inside me changes. This exercise, which I think of as a spiritual discipline, becomes both the cause and the effect of a kind of humility that serves Christian leaders well. The sense of entitlement, so natural when I think of myself as an authority figure, ironically puts me on

a trajectory to irrelevance. Being tutored by experts such as
Spencer and Matt is powerful therapy for this affliction. I still
remember the laughter that erupted when I asked a group of
young pastors *why* they sent text messages. They were not
laughing *with* me. Their amusement stung, but it removed a lens
cap and created an opportunity to help me grasp something so
intuitive for them that I doubt they ever considered the question of *why*. R-mentoring relationships, then, offer a chance to
practice a lifelong discipline of cultivated humility for leaders
willing to break. If we are to reach out effectively in emerging culture, Angie Ward concludes, "The best way to do this is
to become a willing and intentional student of the culture, to
become the humble protégé instead of the mentor."[1] For several
years I taught a seminary class segment on using PowerPoint
until the sad realization that students half my age knew much
more about it than I did. I stepped aside, making space for a new
approach befitting a new time.

2. *R-mentoring changes my methods.* The young are ready to
teach us much more than how to reset malfunctioning MP3
players. Technology serves only as an example of the kinds
of influence they offer. In fact, they sometimes seem unaware of
just how much they know until our questions surface it, suggesting that intuitive knowledge itself represents a form of blindness
for them. For example, I frequently ask young adults what kind
of music they like, and I receive answers such as "I like everything." When I press for details, they describe an iPod packed
with playlists of unlikely companions such as the Beatles, Faith
Hill, U2, and Jay-Z. Gen Y expert Richard Sweeney points out
that "Millennials have no unifying generational music, rap,
classic—anything goes."[2] These choices could be dismissed as
just an artifact of owning an iPod. But multiple conversations
with iPod owners convince me that they also hold a highlight-
reel view of life that presumes the ability to skim off the best
and leave the rest. Asking the young about this preference
quickly forces specific questions, such as, "How do we design

a worship experience for people who demand absolute excellence in everything, but whose musical preferences give a new definition to *eclectic?*" Or, "Is conventional ministry programming even possible for natives of a mash-up culture that combines disparate elements of pop culture into ever-morphing new forms?" The only thing more uncomfortable than facing issues like these is the consequence of not facing them.

3. *R-mentoring energizes me.* As the student of younger leaders, I have experienced the best and happiest part of my ministry over the last half decade. Their availability, honesty, and respectfulness never disappointed. I still feel gratitude toward the young adult congregation that forgave me for destroying their expensive sound board by pouring half a cup of hot coffee into it while clutching desperately at my toppling video camera. In fact, the more inexperience and ignorance I confess (and the supply seems to grow daily), the greater their respectfulness—I suspect because so few older leaders seem willing to admit any type of need. Involvement in this form of relationship often leads to mutual mentoring. With one study finding two-thirds of all age groups expressing a desire for more mentoring in their careers, the reverse form easily taps into this longing for instruction.[3]

No wonder Paul advises believers of all ages in these terms: "Do not rebuke an older man harshly, but exhort him as if he were your father. Treat younger men as brothers, older women as mothers, and younger women as sisters, with absolute purity."[4] Somehow I had always read that passage as *me* admonishing the young, overlooking their function to exhort me. Even fathers need instruction, especially when it comes in the form of life-giving relationships.

In fact, the commitment to learn from the unlikely catalyzes conventional mentoring like little else. I now work with my teachers on problem solving, and choosing their future ministry paths while they continue to instruct me on the present. Along with that of many others, my experience lends support to the idea that R-mentoring offers older leaders a more reliable and enjoyable platform for conventional mentoring than almost anything else. The simple joy of hours spent over coffee learning from these fascinating and unlikely friends keeps leaders fresh by exposing them to personalities and insights they encounter in no other way. The feeling that results might be something like Bob Dylan's lyric: "I was so much older then; I'm younger than that now."

During the research phase for this book, I discovered two communications, one an e-mail and the other a blog post, both referring to 2 Kings 13. A story recorded there tells of the terminally ill prophet Elisha instructing the younger Joash, king of Israel, to fire an arrow out a window as a statement of their mutual faith that God would deliver the nation from a foreign invader. When the king took up the bow and placed the arrow on it, "Elisha put his hands on the king's hands" and together, the unlikely pair fired "the arrow of victory" out an east-facing window in the general direction of the enemy. This compelling illustration was made all the more significant for me by the fact that the e-mail I received about it came from a person my age, while the blog post was authored by a person around thirty. Writing in this context, the elder of the two spoke for both of them in these terms: "Young and old, old and young working together taking advantage of the strengths that both have to offer . . . I am willing to submit to the next generation to learn from them the things I should and trust that I will be able to impart the few things I have gleaned in living life. Life on life investing in the lives of a few. What could one give himself to that would compare to this?"

Two generations, one insight: the almost unexplored power of real collaboration.

Within the next decade, almost half of American CEOs will retire from our major corporations, a statistic that very likely applies to ministry leadership positions as well.[5] The window for influencing the future of the church closes so quickly. But unlikely friends can find a common victory by holding the bow together.

Notes

Introduction

1. Warren, C. "I Spy." *American Way*, Nov. 15, 2007, 58–64.
2. Cindy Goodman (*Miami Herald* correspondent), e-mail, May 21, 2007.
3. Pawson, R. "Mentoring Relationships: An Explanatory Review." ESRC UK Centre for Evidence Based Policy and Practice. *Working Paper 21*(6) [http://www.evidencenetwork .org/Documents/wp21.pdf]; accessed Jan. 5, 2008.

Chapter 1

1. Kawasaki, G. *Art of the Start: The Time-Tested, Battle-Hardened Guide for Anyone Starting Anything.* New York: Portfolio, 2004, 168.
2. Survey of three hundred eighteen-to-thirty-year-olds in the UK by NFO World Group, Aug. 2002, in "What Makes a Brand Cool Anyway?" *Brand Strategy*, Sept. 2002, 36 [http:// www.brandstrateguy.co.uk].
3. Petrecca, L. "The Ads of 2007: Ad-mirable and Ad-dlebrained." *USA Today*, Dec. 31, 2007, 2B [http://www.usatoday.com/money/ advertising/adtrack/2007-12-30-best-worst-ads-2007_N.html]; accessed Jan. 10, 2008.
4. "What Makes a Brand Cool Anyway?"
5. Interview with Andy Ford, Noble and Associates, Springfield, Mo., Dec. 4, 2007.

6. Weir, J. "The Beautiful American Word 'Cool.'" *Rolling Stone*, 2002, 67 (893).

7. Slatalla, M. "omg My Mom Joined Facebook." *New York Times*, June 7, 2007 [http://www.nytimes.com/2007/06/07/fashion/07Cyber.html]; accessed Jan. 5, 2008.

8. Weir.

9. Kane, K. "VP of Cool." *Fast Company*, Oct. 1995, 24 [http://www.fastcompany.com/magazine/01/job1.html]; accessed Jan. 5, 2008.

10. "TOOL: Cool School." *Business Week* [http://images.businessweek.com/ss/07/08/0830_in_short/source/2.htm]; accessed Jan. 5, 2008; "Trend School." Trendcentral.com, Jan. 9, 2006 [http://www.trendcentral.com/trends/trendarticle.asp?tcArticleId=1498&tcCatId=5]; accessed Jan. 5, 2008.

11. Rushkoff, D. "Merchants of Cool." *Frontline* [http://www.pbs.org/wgbh/pages/frontline/shows/cool/]; accessed Dec. 27, 2007.

12. Conley, L. "A Craving for Cool." *FastCompany*, July 2006, (107), 33 [http://www.fastcompany.com/magazine/107/next-essay.html]; accessed Jan. 5, 2008.

13. Armour, S. "Generation Y: They've Arrived with a New Attitude." *USA Today*, Nov. 8, 2005 [http://www.usatoday.com/money/workplace/2005-11-06-gen-y_x.htm]; accessed Dec. 28, 2007.

14. TRU study and Gary Rudman (GTR Consulting), in Goodnow, C. "'Millennials' Thrive on Choice, Instant Results." *Seattle Post Intelligencer*, Mar. 12, 2007 [http://seattlepi.nwsource.com/lifestyle/307124_millennial13.html]; accessed Jan. 5, 2008.

15. Marshall, J. "Reverse Mentoring." The Blog of John 3:16 Marshall. Oct. 13, 2006 [http://www.secondbaptist.org/blog/blog/pastor/]; accessed Jan. 5, 2008.

Chapter 2

1. John Seely Brown quoted in Kruse, K. "Reverse Mentoring: Getting the 'Tech Generation' as Mentors to Your Senior

Team." *HR News and Views*, Sept. 1, 2004 [http://www.jigya saconsulting.com/ezine/index.html]; accessed Jan. 5, 2008.

2. Telephone interview with Anastasia Goodstein, June 25, 2007.

3. Danah Boyd in Kamenetz, A. "The Network Unbound." *Fast Company*, June 2006, (106), 68 [http://www.fastcompany.com/ magazine/106/open_social-networks.html]; accessed Jan. 5, 2008.

4. Boyd, D. "Viewing American Class Divisions Through Facebook and MySpace." June 24, 2007 [http://www.danah.org/ papers/essays/ClassDivisions.html]; accessed Dec. 27, 2007.

5. Florida, R. *Cities and the Creative Class*. New York: Routledge, 2005.

6. Interview with Andy Ford, Noble and Associates. Dec. 4, 2007.

7. Prensky, M. "Capturing the Value of 'Generation Tech' Employees." *Strategy + Business*, June 30, 2004 [http://www .strategy-business.com/press/enewsarticle/enews063004]; accessed Jan. 5, 2008.

Chapter 3

1. James 5:16.

2. Gibson, W. "William Gibson Quotes." [http://thinkexist. com/quotes/william_gibson/]; accessed Dec. 27, 2007.

3. Heads vs. Breakers. "Apathy Is the New Black." Audio CD [http://www.amazon.com/Apathy-New-Black-Heads-Breakers/dp/B0000VV47M]; accessed Dec. 27, 2007.

4. Harlow, C. "They Want More." *Charisma*, Jan. 2008 [http:// www.charismamag.com/display.php?id=16418]; accessed Jan. 30, 2008.

5. 1 Peter 5:3.

6. Gardner, E. "Joel's Words, Dillon's Voice Honor Troops." *USA Today*, Nov. 30, 2007, 1E.

7. "How William Shatner Changed the World." History Channel [http://www.history.com/media.do?mediaType=All

&searchTerm=&action=search&showName=How+William
+Shatner+Changed+the+World]; accessed Jan. 5, 2008.

Chapter 4

1. I am using the term *postmodernity* to refer to the perspective
   that calls into question the assumptions and practices of the
   modern, technological world. Often conceived as a protest
   to modernity, the postmodern view, though variously understood, tends to tilt away from the rational toward the experiential, away from the individualistic toward the communal,
   and away from the scientific toward the artistic. In consum-
   mately postmodern style, this perspective embodies these
   attitudes only selectively, often dipping back into modernity
   as needed. I am indebted to the late Stanley Grenz for many
   of these thoughts. Grenz, S. J. *A Primer on Postmodernism.*
   Grand Rapids, Mich.: Eerdmans, 1996.
2. Matthew 15:13.
3. Matthew 23:6–7.
4. Senge, P. *The Fifth Discipline: The Art & Practice of the
   Learning Organization.* New York: Doubleday, 1990, 182.
5. Duffy, D. "Drivers Ed." *CIO* [http://www.darwinmag.com/
   read/080101/ed.html]; accessed Sept. 30, 2005.
6. Miller, M. "Out of the Minds of Babes." Reprinted from
   the *Los Angeles Times*, 2001. *Generation Yes* [http://www
   .genyes.com/search.php?q=usual]; accessed Jan. 5, 2008.
7. Deal, J. *Retiring the Generation Gap: How Employees Young
   and Old Can Find Common Ground.* San Francisco: Jossey-
   Bass, 2006.
8. Don Tapscott in Tristram, C. "Turning the Tables." RedHerring.
   com, Aug. 21, 2000 [http://www.redherring.com/]; accessed Jan.
   5, 2008.
9. Telephone interview with Anastasia Goodstein, June 25,
   2007 [http://www.ypulse.com].
10. 1 Samuel 18:8–11; 19:9; 20:32–34.

11. Lewis, C. S. *The Four Loves*. New York: Harcourt Brace Jovanovich, 1960, 70–73, 77–79.

12. David McQuillen in Wylie, I. "Talk to Our Customers? Are You Crazy?" *Fast Company*, July-Aug. 2006, (107), 70 [http://www.fastcompany.com/magazine/107/business-at-its-best.html]; accessed Jan. 5, 2008.

Chapter 5

1. "Infolust." Trendwatching.com [http://www.trendwatching.com/trends/infolust.html]; accessed Dec. 7, 2007.

2. Kornblum, J. "Americans Will Devote Half Their Lives to Forms of Media Next Year." *USA Today*, Dec. 15, 2006, 6A; J. T. Johnson, president, Nemertes Research, a business technology analysis firm, in Lieberman, D. "Video, Interactivity Could Ensnare Web Users by 2010." *USA Today*, Nov. 19, 2007, 1B; Amazon search Dec. 2007.

3. George Barna in Stafford, T. "The Third Coming of George Barna." *Christianity Today*, Aug. 5, 2002 [http://www.christianitytoday.com/ct/2002/august5/1.32.html]; accessed Dec. 7, 2007.

4. Goldfarb, Z. "Maryland Joins Megacomputer 'Cloud' Project." *Washington Post*, Oct. 9, 2007 [http://www.washingtonpost.com/wp-dyn/content/article/2007/10/08/AR2007100801521.html]; accessed Dec. 6, 2007.

5. Leslie in Goodnow, C. "'Millennials' Thrive on Choice, Instant Results." *Seattle Post Intelligencer*, Mar. 12, 2007 [http://seattlepi.nwsource.com/lifestyle/307124_millennial13.html]; accessed Jan. 5, 2008.

6. Christie, A., and others. "Scaffolding Graduate Students' Learning Through Collaboration with Gen Y Students." NECC 2004, 10 [http://www.alicechristie.com/pubs/Christie-Scaffolding.pdf]; accessed Jan. 5, 2008.

7. Goodnow.

8. Paul Saffo in Kornblum.

9. Christie and others, 8, 10.

10. 1 Kings 3:5–14.

11. Ebersole, J., dean, Boston University Division of Extended Education, in Fitzgerald, B. "Lifelong Learning Is Goal of New Division of Extended Education." *B. U. Bridge*, Aug. 31, 2001, 5(3) [http://www.bu.edu/bridge/archive/2001/08-31/exed.html]; accessed Dec. 7, 2007; Ebersole, J. "The Future of Graduate Education." *University Business*, Aug. 2004 [http://www.universitybusiness.com/viewarticle.aspx?articleid=527]; accessed Dec. 7, 2007.

12. Weil, E. "The Future Is Younger Than You Think." *Fast Company*, Apr. 1997, (8), 93 [http://www.fastcompany.com/magazine/08/kids.html]; accessed Dec. 7, 2007.

13. Towns, J. *Reverse Mentoring: What My Students Taught Me*. Longwood, Fla.: Xulon Press, 2005, ix.

Chapter 6

1. Pawson, R. "Mentoring Relationships: An Explanatory Review." ESRC UK Centre for Evidence Based Policy and Practice. *Working Paper 21*, 6 [http://www.evidencenetwork.org/Documents/wp21.pdf]; accessed Jan. 5, 2008.

2. Browne, H. A. "Time to Build Bridges." *Signal Magazine*, Aug. 2006 [http://www.afcea.org/signal/]; accessed Jan. 5, 2008.

3. Schlichting, R. "Man to Man." *Worship Well* blog, Apr. 24, 2007 [http://worshipwell.blogspot.com/2007/04/man-to-man.html]; accessed Dec. 15, 2007; Wood, B. Comment posted on *Worship Well* blog [https://www.blogger.com/comment.g?blogID=33569806&postID=7273893053914094278&pli=1]; accessed Dec. 15, 2007.

4. Horris, MC Lars. "iGeneration" [http://www.azlyrics.com/lyrics/mclars/igeneration.html]; accessed Dec. 15, 2007; [http://mclars.com/v2/].

5. [http://www.myspace.com/mclars]; accessed Dec. 15, 2007.

6. Young, A. "When Cultures Collide." *The Economist*, Dec. 21, 2000.

7. D. Cantu, *HBR* senior editor, interview with Edgar Schein. "Edgar H. Schein: The Anxiety of Learning—The Darker Side of Organizational Learning." *Harvard Business School Working Knowledge*, Apr. 15, 2002 [http://hbswk.hbs.edu/archive/2888.html]; accessed Jan. 5, 2007.

8. Schrage, M. "My Customer/My Co-Inventor." *Strategy + Business*, Aug. 31, 2006 [http://www.strategy-business.com/enewsarticle/enews083106?pg=all]; accessed Jan. 5, 2008.

9. Timberlake, C. "Upstart Execs Teach Older Dogs New Tricks." CareerJournalEurope.com, n.d. [http://www.careerjournaleurope.com/myc/officelife/20010327-timberlake.html]; accessed Jan. 5, 2008.

10. Picanol. *2001 Annual Report* [http://www.picanolgroup.com/NR/rdonlyres/5A62FB3F-C86F-4281-9077-737153846AEC/0/PICANOL_ANNUAL_REPORT_29_04.pdf]; accessed Jan. 5, 2008.

11. Keveny, B. "'Lost' Soul Mates." *USA Today*, Sept. 29, 2006, 1E.

12. Interview with Andy Ford, Nobel and Associates, Springfield, Mo., Dec. 4, 2007.

Chapter 7

1. Colossians 4:5–6.

2. Sutton, R. *Weird Ideas That Work*. New York: Free Press, 2001, 71.

3. Mark 12:37.

4. Gallup, G., Jr. "Who Will Lead the US Religious Revival?" *Gallup Poll Tuesday Briefing*. Nov. 26, 2002, 96.

5. Kyle Smith interview with Sheryl Crow. "Sheryl Crow in the Hot Seat." FoxNews.com, Oct. 1, 2005 [http://www.foxnews.com/story/0,2933,170990,00.html]; accessed Jan. 5, 2008.

6. Takazawa, T. "Listening Shops." *Japan Stories* (podcast hosted by Peter Thomson), Feb. 19, 2007 [http://www.thomsontimes

.com/podcast/2007/02/listening-shops.html]; accessed Dec. 1, 2007.

7. I am indebted to Doug Oss, professor of preaching at the Assemblies of God Theological Seminary, for this expression.

8. Hunter, T. "Off the Map Update" (e-mail newsletter), Dec. 11, 2007.

9. 2 Samuel 16:5–14.

10. 1 Corinthians 13:1.

11. Stetzer, E. "Evangelism as Answering People's Questions." *CMR Insights*, Apr. 28, 2006 [http://www.namb.net/site/apps/nl/content2.asp?c=9qKILUOzEpH&b=2027651&ct=3318269]; accessed Jan. 5, 2008.

Chapter 8

1. David Siegel in Mieszkowski, K. "Web Sight—Let Your Customers Lead." *Fast Company*, Mar. 2000, (33), 210 [http://www.fastcompany.com/magazine/33/siegel.html]; accessed Jan. 5, 2008.

2. Prensky, M. "Capturing the Value of 'Generation Tech' Employees." *Strategy + Business*, June 30, 2004 [http://www.strategy-business.com/press/enewsarticle/enews063004]; accessed Jan. 5, 2008.

3. Mayer, I. *[EPM] Datafile* (e-mail newsletter), May 21, 2007, 2(22) *[EML] Datafile*, *Entertainment Marketing Letters* (e-mail newsletter), Oct. 25, 2007, 1(10).

4. Kinney, M., vice president, research and planning, Integer, in Kelly, B. "Past the Pedestal." *Promo*, Dec. 1, 2003 [http://promomagazine.com/mag/marketing_past_pedestal/]; accessed Jan. 5, 2008.

5. Patrick Dixon in Muller, G. "By 2012 Today's Teens Will Rule." *Business Day*, June 13, 2007 [http://www.theage.com.au/news/business/by-2012-todays-teens-will-rule/2007/06/12/1181414299813.html]; accessed Jan. 5, 2008.

6. Tushar, T., Jr. "A Letter to the Preacher" (blog). Oct. 27, 2004 [http://fracturedreflections.blogspot.com/2004/10/letter-to-preacher.html].
7. 1 Corinthians 15:1.
8. Tushar.
9. Kinney.

Chapter 9

1. Vancheri, B. "Networks Turn from X to Y in Search for Next Generation." *Pittsburgh Post Gazette*, May 4, 1999 [http://seattlepi.nwsource.com/tv/teen04.shtml]; accessed Jan. 9, 2008.
2. Goodnow, C. "'Millennials' Thrive on Choice, Instant Results." *Seattle Post Intelligencer*, Mar. 12, 2007 [http://seattlepi.nwsource.com/lifestyle/307124_millennial13.html]; accessed Jan. 5, 2008.
3. Goodnow.
4. M. Useem, interviewed by Brook Manville. "Leading Up to 'Leading Up': An Interview with Wharton Professor Mike Useem." *LineZine: Leader Learning*, Fall 2000 [http://www.linezine.com/6.1/interviews/mubmlutlu.htm]; accessed Jan. 9, 2008.
5. Tom Peters in George, K. L. "The Cool School of Tom Peters." *Executive Update*, April 2001 [http://www.asaecenter.org/PublicationsResources/articledetail.cfm?itemnumber=13038]; accessed Jan. 9, 2008.
6. Hebrews 11:26.
7. Johnson, A. R. "An Anthropological Approach to the Study of Leadership: Lessons Learned on Improving Leadership Practice." *Transformation*, July, Oct. 2007, *24*(3, 4), 213–221.
8. Triple Creek Associates. "Learning to Compete in a Knowledge Economy." *Mentoring Article Review*, 2006, 2 [http://www.3creek.com/resources/research/AR_KnowledgeEconomy.pdf]; accessed Jan. 9, 2008; from Schramm, J. "Learning to Compete in a Knowledge Economy." SHRM Research. *Workplace Visions*, 2005, (3), 1–8 [http://www.shrm.org/trends/visions/3issue2005/WorkplaceVisions3.pdf]; accessed Jan. 9, 2008.

9. 2 Corinthians 4:7.

10. Kawasaki, G. *Art of the Start: The Time-Tested, Battle-Hardened Guide for Anyone Starting Anything.* New York: Portfolio, 2004, 84, 85.

11. "Customer Made." Trendwatching.Com, e-mail newsletter, May 2005 [http://www.trendwatching.com/newsletter/previ ous_26.html]; accessed Jan. 9, 2008.

12. Tom Peters in George.

13. Acts 6:5.

Chapter 10

1. B. Welch in Turner, C. "Draper Calls for Revolution at Younger Leaders Summit." *Lifeway* [http://www.lifeway.com/lwc/article_ main_page/0,1703,A%253D160296%2526M%253D50011,00. html]; accessed Jan. 9, 2008.

2. Tapscott, D., Ticoll, D., and Lowry, A. "Human Capital in the Business Web." *Workforce Management,* June 5, 2000 [http://www.workforce.com/archive/feature/22/24/30/index. php?ht=%22human%20capital%20in%20the%20business% 20web%22%20%22human%20capital%20in%20the%20bus iness%20web%22]; accessed Jan. 9, 2008.

3. Shaffer, K. "New Technology Changes Culture." *Church Relevance,* July 2007, (21) [http://churchrelevance.com/ newsletter/new-technology-changes-culture/]; accessed Jan. 9, 2008.

4. 1 Corinthians 12:25.

5. 2006 Randstad USA survey, in Tang, C. "The Great Divide." *Insight Magazine,* Jan.-Feb. 2007 [http://www.icpas.org/hc -insight.aspx?id=204]; accessed Jan. 9, 2008.

6. Conn, H. M., and Ortiz, M. *Urban Ministry: The Kingdom, the City, and the People of God.* Downers Grove, Ill.: InterVarsity, 2001, 279.

7. Higgins, M. C. "Too Old to Learn?" *Harvard Business Review,* Nov.-Dec. 2000, 7.

8. Conn and Ortiz, 275–276.

9. Robin Throckmorton in Grady, M. "Each Generation Can Teach Others New Ways to Work." *East Valley Tribune*, May 8, 2007 [http://www.eastvalleytribune.com/story/89262]; accessed Jan. 9, 2008. See also Throckmorton, R., and Gravett, L. *Bridging the Generation Gap*. Franklin Lakes, N.J.: Career Press, 2007.

Chapter 11

1. Tom Kelley in Goodman, C. K. "Reverse Mentoring Taps into Fount of Knowledge." *South Coast Today*, Apr. 25, 2006 [http://archive.southcoasttoday.com/daily/05-06/05-02-06/07career.html]; accessed Jan. 9, 2008.

2. Matt Starcevich in Henricks, M. "Kids These Days: Senior Staff Hopelessly Out of Date? Younger Mentors Can Help Them Keep Up." *Entrepreneur*, May 2002 [http://findarticles.com/p/articles/mi_m0DTI/is_5_30/ai_96892214]; accessed Jan. 9, 2008.

3. Kanter, R. M. *Evolve! Succeeding in the Digital Culture of Tomorrow*. Cambridge, Mass.: Harvard Business School Press, 2001, 60–61.

4. Chang, J. "Backward Learning." *Sales and Marketing Management*, Jan. 4, 2004, 156(1), 24 [http://www.allbusiness.com/marketing-advertising/4289365-1.html]; accessed Jan. 9, 2008.

5. Jerry Wind in Carter, T. "Recipe for Growth." *ABA Journal*, Apr. 2004, 90(4), 85 [http://www.abajournal.com/magazine/recipe_for_growth/print/]; accessed Jan. 9, 2008.

6. Starcevich, M. M. "What Is Unique About Reverse Mentoring, Survey Results" [http://www.coachingandmentoring.com/reversementoringresults.html]; accessed Jan. 9, 2008.

7. Miller, M. "Out of the Minds of Babes." Reprinted from the *Los Angeles Times*, 2001 [http://www.genyes.org/news/mindsofbabes]; accessed Jan. 9, 2008.

8. 1 Peter 5:3.
9. Henderson J., and Casper, M. *Jim & Casper Go to Church.* Carol Stream, Ill.: Barna/Tyndale, 2007.
10. Robin Torgerson in Joseph, J. "Upward Mentoring: The Wharton Fellows in eBusiness." *Wharton Leadership Digest,* Jan. 2001, 5(4) [http://leadership.wharton.upenn.edu/ digest/01-01.shtml#Upward%20Mentoring:%20%20The%20 Wharton%20Fellows%20in%20eBusiness%20%C2%A0].
11. Wind, J. "Too Old to Learn?" *Harvard Business Review,* Nov.-Dec. 2000, 11.
12. Triple Creek Associates. "Marginal Mentoring: The Effects of Type of Mentor, Quality of Relationship, and Program Design on Work and Career Attitudes." *Mentoring Article Review* [http:// www.3creek.com/resources/research/AR_MarginalMentoring. pdf]; accessed Jan. 9, 2008. Review of Ragins, B. R., Cotton, J. L., and Miller, J. S. "Marginal Mentoring: The Effects of Type of Mentor, Quality of Relationship, and Program Design on Work and Career Attitudes." *Academy of Management Journal,* Dec. 2000.
13. Triple Creek Associates.
14. Triple Creek Associates. "Why Mentoring Programs and Relationships Fail." *Mentoring Article Review,* 2006 [http:// www.linkageinc.com/company/news_events/link_learn_ enewsletter/archive/2002/12_02_mentoring_clutterbuck. aspx]. Review of Clutterbuck, D. "Why Mentoring Programs and Relationships Fail." *Link & Learn eNewsletter,* Dec. 2002.
15. Tom Kelley in Goodman.
16. Balu, R. "Listen Up." *Fast Company,* Apr. 2000, 34, 304.
17. Triple Creek Associates. "Mentors Without Borders: Global Mentors Can Give Employees a Different Perspective on Business Matters." *Mentoring Article Review,* 2006 [http:// www.3creek.com/resources/research/AR_Mentors_wo_ Borders.pdf]; accessed Jan. 5, 2008. Review of Overman, S. "Mentors Without Borders: Global Mentors Can Give

Employees a Different Perspective on Business Matters." *HR Magazine*, Mar. 2004, 83–86.

18. Podmolik, M. E. "Mentor Match Found Online." *Chicago Tribune*, May 14, 2007 [http://www.mediapro.com/html/Services/mentoring/articles/MentorMatchFoundOnline.html]; accessed Jan. 9, 2008; Frank Morgan in Overman. Triple Creek Associates, review of mentoring article [http://www.3creek.com/resources/research/AR_Mentors_wo_Borders.pdf].

19. Podmolik.

20. Tom Peters quoted in Lancaster, L. C., and Stillman, D. *When Generations Collide*. New York: Collins Business, 2002, 334.

Chapter 12

1. Creps, E. *Off-Road Disciplines: Spiritual Adventures of Missional Leaders*. San Francisco: Jossey-Bass, 2006.

2. Survey by Procter & Gamble in Mayer, I. *[EMP] Datafile* (e-mail newsletter), Dec. 3, 2007, 2(50) [http://www.epmcom.com/].

3. Creps, E., "Worldview Therapy." In M. Yaconelli (ed.), *Stories of Emergence: Moving from Absolute to Authentic*. Grand Rapids, Mich.: Zondervan/Youth Specialties, 2003, 147–163.

4. Kanter, R. M. *Evolve! Succeeding in the Digital Culture of Tomorrow*. Cambridge, Mass.: Harvard Business School Press, 2001, 61, 64.

5. Goodman, C. K. "The Work/Life Balancing Act: Do You Need a Reverse Mentor?" (blog). MiamiHerald.com, Mar. 13, 2006 [http://worklifebalancingact.blogspot.com/2006_03_01_archive.html]; accessed Jan. 9, 2008.

6. Y. Fritzsche, researcher, Psydata, in "Know Future." *The Economist*, Dec. 21, 2000 [http://www.economist.com/surveys/displayStory.cfm?Story_id=455168]; accessed Jan. 9, 2008.

Epilogue

1. Ward, A. "Reverse Mentoring: The New Learning Curve Is from the Bottom Up." LeadershipJournal.net, Aug. 24, 2004 [http://www.christianitytoday.com/leaders/newsletter/2004/cln40824.html]; accessed Jan. 9, 2008.

2. Richard Sweeney in Goodnow, C. "'Millennials Thrive on Choice, Instant Results." *Seattle Post Intelligencer*, Mar. 12, 2007 [http://seattlepi.nwsource.com/lifestyle/307124_millennial13.html]; accessed Jan. 9, 2008.

3. Lancaster, L. C., and Stillman, D. *When Generations Collide*. New York: Collins Business, 2002, 335.

4. 1 Timothy 5:1–2.

5. Fontaine, M. "U.S. Best at Grooming Leaders of the Future." *Management-Issues*, Jan. 4, 2007 [http://www.management-issues.com/2007/4/25/research/leadership-begins-at-school.asp]; accessed Jan. 9, 2008.

Acknowledgments

The practice of reverse mentoring began so informally and so unobtrusively in my life that I have trouble defining its starting point. Being in relationship with a number of young leaders, I thought it just seemed natural to ask them about their lives. Little did I know that simple curiosity would lead to startling discoveries about me and my own need to change and grow. So, in one sense, the list of authors runs into the dozens if I count all the people who answered all those questions and with whom I shared so much coffee. All I have done here is chronicle the experience of these relationships and the very generous people who made them available to me. Without people like Joel, Glen, Tony, Adam, Eric, Mark, Justin, Dan, Curt, Donnie, and so many others, I literally do not know who or what I would be today, and I am certain that our church-starting project in Berkeley would not be happening.

However, the best part of the RM journey has been sharing it with Janet, my partner in life and ministry. We have both benefited so much from the influence of our young friends.

The opportunity to partner for a second time with Leadership Network and Jossey-Bass has been one of the very best parts of working on this project. I am grateful to Greg Ligon, Stephanie Plagens, and my agent, Mark Sweeney of Leadership Network, for the vision to serve leaders that makes books like this possible. My friends at Jossey-Bass have also been a joy to work with. Andrea, Alison, Natalie, and Erik have been great partners. Special thanks are due to Sheryl Fullerton, for her constant encouragement, especially one afternoon in Seattle when I really needed it, and her flawless instincts for shaping words into thoughts and thoughts into books. She deserves a great deal of credit for whatever merit this book possesses. Finally, I want to express gratitude to Thomas Finnegan and Tracy Harrington, whose editorial Jedi powers continue to amaze while immunizing my text against error in all its forms.

The actual composition of the text proved challenging during a time when Janet and I were transitioning from my role at the Assemblies of God Theological Seminary into church starting. The time pressure was extreme. But our friends kept us encouraged, including making their homes available when we had sold our own to begin work on our church start-up. In particular, I want to thank Byron and Lois Klaus, in whose basement I wrote about a third of this book, and Jay and Cheryl Taylor, who provided the home where I wrote the other two-thirds. This project has truly been a team sport.

Our move to church starting in Berkeley will afford the best possible laboratory for reverse mentoring. We will have the opportunity to test the ideas in this book perhaps farther than we ever imagined. The practice of R-mentoring is no guarantee of fruitfulness, but neither would I want to begin this new ministry without it.

About the Author

Earl Creps has spent several years on the road studying missional congregations and connecting with young leaders. He brings to this research a background as a pastor, having led three churches (one Boomer, one Builder, and one Gen X); a consultant, having served as his denomination's national adult ministries consultant; and an educator, teaching on mission in emerging culture for the Assemblies of God Theological Seminary. Earl has earned a Ph.D. in communication (Northwestern University) and a doctor of ministry (AGTS). Currently, he is team leader for the Berkeley Church Planting Project through Assemblies of God US Missions. Earl is the author of numerous articles and adult study courses, and a speaker for seminars and conferences. His book *Off-Road Disciplines: Spiritual Adventures of Missional Leaders* was published by Leadership Network/Jossey-Bass in 2006.

Index

Also by Earl Creps

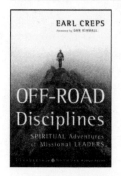

Off-Road Disciplines
Spiritual Adventures of Missional Leaders

Earl Creps

Hardcover
ISBN: 978-0-7879-8520-2

"*As a well-traveled explorer of the Church over many years, Earl offers more than a description of the latest cool topics in leadership. . . . You hold something that is rich, cured, and aged to sink into your mind and heart in a way that couldn't happen without breadth of experience behind it. This isn't a book about a quick fix to break an attendance barrier, or bringing new music or a new design for a worship gathering. It isn't about how to give better sermons. Earl writes about the most important thing he has discovered in all his exploring of the Church: the life of the missional leader and its effect on a missional organization.*"

—from the Foreword by **Dan Kimball**

In *Off-Road Disciplines,* Earl Creps reveals that the on-road practices of prayer and Bible reading should be bolstered by the other kinds of encounters with God that occur unexpectedly—complete with the bumps and bruises that happen when you go "off-road." Becoming an off-road leader requires the cultivation of certain spiritual disciplines that allow the presence of the Holy Spirit to arrange your interior life. Earl Creps explores twelve central spiritual disciplines—six personal and six organizational—that Christian leaders of all ages and denominations need if they are to change themselves and their churches to reach out to the culture around them.

Earl Creps explores each of these off-road disciplines and shows how to make them part of normal daily life so that they can have a transformative effect. Creps provides a map of the cultural terrain leaders must navigate and offers insight on the ways in which the process of personal spiritual formation can lead to changes in organizations.

Visit the Leadership Network Website
www.leadnet.org

Other Books of Interest

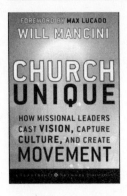

Church Unique

How Missional Leaders Cast Vision, Capture
Culture, and Create Movement

Will Mancini

Hardcover
ISBN: 978-0-7879-9679-3

---

*"There is a screaming need today for leaders who will rise above quick fixes
and generic approaches. Now, Will Mancini has brought an indispensable
book to the church leader's toolbox, providing a thoughtful and creative process that will galvanize your team to unleash God's vision for your church."*

—**Howard Hendricks,** chairman, Center for Christian Leadership;
distinguished professor, Dallas Theological Seminary

In **Church Unique,** church consultant Will Mancini offers an
approach for rethinking what it means to lead with clarity as a vision-
ary. Mancini explains that each church has a culture that reflects its
particular values, thoughts, attitudes, and actions, and shows how
church leaders can unlock their church's individual DNA and unleash
their congregation's one-of-a-kind potential.

Mancini explores the pitfalls churches often fall into in their attempt
to grow and explores a new model for vision casting and church
growth that has been tested with leaders in all kinds of congregations,
including mainline, evangelical, small, and large. The practices and
ideas outlined in **Church Unique** will help leaders develop missional
teams, articulate unique strategies, unpack the baggage of institution-
alism, and live fully into their vision.

Whether leading a megachurch or church plant, a multisite or mainline, a ministry or parachurch, **Church Unique** will provide inspiration
as a practical guide for leading into the future. There is a better way.

WILL MANCINI, a former pastor, is the founder of Auxano, a
national consulting group that works with traditional and emerging
churches and ministries of all types around the country. Their mission
is to navigate leaders through growth challenges with vision clarity
(www.auxano.com).

Other Books of Interest

The Tangible Kingdom
Creating Incarnational Community

Hugh Halter • Matt Smay

Hardcover
ISBN: 978-0-470-18897-2

"Among increasing numbers of faithful, conservative, Bible-believing Christians, an important shift is beginning to occur. These aren't wild-eyed radicals; they're solid, established church leaders and members who are asking new questions because deep within they discern that something is wrong with the status quo. Hugh and Matt have been through this shift, and offer wise counsel for a way forward."

—**Brian McLaren,** author, *A New Kind of Christian* Trilogy and *Everything Must Change*

Written for those who are trying to nurture authentic faith communities and for those who have struggled to retain their faith, **The Tangible Kingdom** offers theological answers and real-life stories that demonstrate how the best ancient church practices can re-emerge in today's culture, through any church of any size.

The Tangible Kingdom outlines an innovative model for creating thriving grass-roots faith communities, offering new hope for church leaders, pastors, church planters, and churchgoers who are looking for practical new ways to re-orient their lives to fit God's mission today.

HUGH HALTER is a specialist with Church Resource Ministries and the national director of Missio, a global network of missional leaders and church planters. He is also lead architect of Adullam, a congregational network of incarnational communities in Denver, Colorado (www.adullamdenver.com).

MATT SMAY codirects both Missio and Adullam and specializes in helping existing congregations move toward mission. Halter and Smay direct the MCAP, "missional church apprenticeship practicum," an international training network for incarnational church planters, pastors, and emerging leaders (www.missio.us).

Other Books of Interest

Organic Church
Growing Faith Where Life Happens

Neil Cole

Hardcover
ISBN: 978-0-7879-8129-7

"I heartily recommend this book. It is packed with deep insights; you will find no fluff in it. Among the books on church planting, it offers a rare combination of attributes: it is biblical and well written, its model has proven effective, and it is authored by a practitioner rather than an observer or an ivory-tower theoretician."

—**Curtis Sergeant,** director of church planting, Saddleback Church

Leaders and laypeople everywhere are realizing that they need new and more powerful ways to help them spread God's Word. According to international church starter and pastor Neil Cole, if we want to connect with young people and those who are not coming to church, we must go where people congregate.

Cole shows readers how to plant the seeds of the Kingdom of God in the places where life happens and where culture is formed—restaurants, bars, coffeehouses, parks, locker rooms, and neighborhoods. *Organic Church* offers a hands-on guide for demystifying this new model of church and shows the practical aspects of implementing it.

Visit the Leadership Network Website, www.leadnet.org, for more innovative resources and information. You can find more resources on organic church planting at www.cmaresources.org.

NEIL COLE is a church starter and pastor, and founder and executive director of Church Multiplication Associates, which has helped start over seven hundred churches in thirty-two states and twenty-three nations in six years. He is an international speaker and the author of *Cultivating a Life for God*.

Other Books of Interest

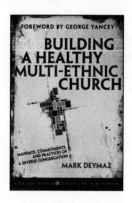

Building a Healthy Multi-Ethnic Church
Mandate, Commitments and Practices of a
Diverse Congregation

Mark DeYmaz

Hardcover
ISBN: 978-0-7879-9551-5

For more than one hundred years, eleven o'clock on Sunday morning has been called the most segregated hour in the land. Despite the integration of public schools, the workplace, and neighborhoods, the local church stubbornly clings to homogeneity. As America grows more and more diverse, the local church will be forced to adapt in order to remain relevant and effective. Good intentions, however, are not enough to inspire systemic change.

Building a Healthy Multi-Ethnic Church explains why the growing fascination with multi-ethnic churches must not be focused on racial reconciliation but on reconciling individuals to Jesus Christ and on reconciling local congregations of faith with the inclusive nature of the New Testament Church.

Through personal stories and a thorough analysis of the biblical text, Mark DeYmaz, pastor of one of the most successful multi-ethnic churches in the country, provides the theological mandate for the multi-ethnic church and outlines seven core commitments required to bring it about. Writing from his comprehensive experience in planting, growing, and encouraging more ethnically diverse communities of faith, he demonstrates why the most effective way to advance the Gospel in the twenty-first century will be through strong and vital multi-ethnic churches.

MARK DEYMAZ is pastor of the Mosaic Church of Central Arkansas, a multi-ethnic and economically diverse church where men and women from more than thirty nations currently worship God together as one. Formerly, he served on Little Rock's Racial and Cultural Diversity Commission and he is a cofounder of the Mosaix Global Network, an organization dedicated to enlisting and equipping leaders intent on the development of multi-ethnic churches throughout America and beyond.

Other Books of Interest

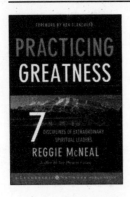

Practicing Greatness
7 Disciplines of Extraordinary Spiritual Leaders

Reggie McNeal
Foreword by Ken Blanchard

Hardcover
ISBN: 978-0-7879-7753-5

"The depth and breadth of wisdom in this book is just short of unbelievable. Good leaders aspiring to be great leaders will do well to read this book and allow it to probe and shape their lives."

—**Bill Easum,** Easum, Bandy & Associates

How do good spiritual leaders become great leaders?

Based on his experience coaching and mentoring thousands of Christian leaders across a broad spectrum of ministry settings, best-selling leadership expert and consultant Reggie McNeal helps spiritual leaders understand that they will self-select into or out of greatness.

In this important book, McNeal shows how great spiritual leaders are committed consciously and intentionally to seven spiritual disciplines, habits of heart and mind that shape both their character and competence: self-awareness, self-management, a lifelong commitment to self-development through personal growth and learning, a sense of mission, learning to make great decisions, the commitment to live in community, and the intentional practice of solitude and contemplation.

Practicing Greatness goes beyond mere clichés and inspirational thoughts to be a hard-hitting resource for leaders who aspire to go from being just good enough to being a great leader who blesses others.

REGGIE MCNEAL is the director of leadership development for the South Carolina Baptist Convention. Through his extensive coaching roles, he has been devoted to helping leaders understand and practice true leadership greatness. Mr. McNeal is the author of *Revolution in Leadership: Training Apostles for Tomorrow's Church, A Work of Heart: Understanding How God Shapes Spiritual Leaders* and the best-selling *The Present Future: Six Tough Questions for the Church.*